✽Teaching,
✽Coaching, and
✽Learning

TENNIS:

an annotated bibliography

by
DENNIS J. PHILLIPS

Robinson Public Library District
606 North Jefferson Street
Robinson, IL 62454-2699

The Scarecrow Press, Inc.
Metuchen, N.J., & London
1989

The dissertation titles and abstracts contained here are published with permission of University Microfilms International, publishers of Dissertation Abstracts International (copyright © 1968-1988 by University Microfilms International), and may not be reproduced without their prior permission. Copies of the dissertations may be obtained by addressing your request to: University Microfilms International, 300 North Zeeb Road, Ann Arbor, Michigan 48106, or by telephoning (toll-free) 1-800-521-3042.

British Library Cataloguing-in-Publication data available

Library of Congress Cataloging-in-Publication Data

Phillips, Dennis J., 1947-
  Teaching, coaching, and learning tennis : an annotated bibliography / by Dennis J. Phillips.
     p.   cm.
  Includes indexes.
  ISBN 0-8108-2254-7
  1. Tennis--Bibliography. 2. Tennis--United States--Bibliography. I. Title.
Z7514.T3P47   1989
[GV995]
016.796342'0973--dc20   89-10534

Copyright © 1989 by Dennis J. Phillips
Manufactured in the United States of America

Printed on acid-free paper

TO JERRY

CONTENTS

	Acknowledgments	vii
	Introduction	ix
I.	Bibliography	1
II.	Title Index	143
III.	Subject Index	167

ACKNOWLEDGMENTS

I would like to thank several people who contributed significantly in the completion of this project. The USTA Center for Education and Recreational Tennis provided funding and guidance during the initial stage of my research. The cooperation and assistance of the research staff at the International Tennis Hall of Fame resulted in locating many of the early books written on tennis. Kathy Romig of the Penn State Allentown campus worked tirelessly in processing hundreds of interlibrary loan requests and followed up relentlessly on elusive materials. Nancy Eberle worked diligently for long hours while transposing my original drafts and a plethora of editorial changes into a machine-readable database file. Finally, I would like to acknowledge the coaches, players, students, and other people who have throughout the years shared with me the many rewarding benefits of tennis. Thank you all.

Introduction

Historians trace the origin of modern lawn tennis to the 13th-century French game known as jeu de paume, "game of the palm." From this game, court tennis or real (royal) tennis evolved as an indoor game in which an asymmetrical wooden racket was used to strike white cloth balls. Court tennis is still played today in England, France, Australia, and the United States.

Major Walter Clopton Wingfield of North Wales is credited with the invention of lawn tennis. Although Wingfield was unsuccessful in his attempt to copyright the game itself which he called "Sphairistike," he obtained a patent for the game's original hourglass-shaped court in 1874. In that same year, Harrison and Sons of London published Wingfield's first book of lawn tennis rules, The Major's Game of Lawn Tennis. According to some tennis historians, the sport was introduced in America in 1874 when Mary E. Outerbridge of New York returned from a trip to Bermuda with a set of rackets, balls, and a net. The popularity of tennis quickly spread to other cities including Boston, Newport, Philadelphia, and New Orleans. In 1881, the United States National Lawn Tennis Association was founded and the first official U.S. National Championship was played on the carefully manicured grass courts at the Newport Casino in Rhode Island.

Since that time many changes have occurred in the sport. In 1968, the open era of tennis began which permitted amateur and professional players to compete in the same tournaments. Shortly thereafter, tennis became a big business. Today the game is played on a variety of natural and synthetic court surfaces. Players travel to all parts of the world each year to compete in dozens of tournaments for millions of dollars in prize money. Blended composite materials are shaped to create rackets designed to give players maximum power and control. Sophisticated diets and intensive fitness programs are scientifically developed for men and women on the international circuit. Young players are enrolled in tennis camps, clinics, academies, and sports institutes to optimize their tennis skills. Highly acclaimed coaches work daily with the most promising of these players.

With all the changes tennis has endured over the past twenty years, the fundamentals of teaching and learning the game remain the same. However, advanced tennis techniques, strategies, tactics, and training methods are constantly under study. The latest teaching theories espoused by professional tennis instructors are found in recently published literature. Readers are advised to select materials from this bibliography according to their research goals.

This bibliography is intended to promote the use of tennis literature by researchers, teaching professionals, coaches, physical education personnel, players, and students of tennis. Its purpose is to identify and organize a specific body of literature within the broader range of the sport's bibliographic parameters. To that end, research works and serious writings on the scientific, technical, physiological, psychological, and health aspects of tennis are emphasized. Many of the items listed are written by or contain contributions from the world's top players, strategists, and teachers.

Published books, theses, pamphlets, and unpublished studies produced in the United States between the years 1968-1988 are covered. Several classic works written by such former tennis greats as Bill Tilden, Maureen Connolly, and others are also listed. A select number of foreign imprints have been included but these titles are limited to those written in English. The bibliography is restricted to publications devoted to teaching, coaching, learning, and playing the sport of tennis. It does not cover tennis biographies, histories, court construction manuals, fictional works, or other literature which is not pedagogical in its focus. Nor does it list books or other materials in which tennis is only one of many sports discussed.

Arrangement of the bibliography is alphabetical by author's last name. There are _see_ and _see also_ references for added author entries. Full bibliographic information appears for most citations: author, title, edition, place of publication, publisher, date of publication, number of pages, Library of Congress number, and ISBN. Additional information has been provided for primary sources, e.g., ERIC documents contain the ED order number and theses include the University Microfilms International order number. A descriptive annotation follows each bibliographic entry. Following the annotation, special features of the work are listed such as color photographs, diagrams, bibliography, index, and glossary. A title and subject index are also included.

Documents available from ERIC may be obtained from the ERIC Document Reproduction Service, 3900 Wheeler Avenue, Alexandria, Virginia 22304 or in libraries subscribing to the ERIC microfiche collection.

The dissertation titles and abstracts contained in this bibliography are published with permission of University Microfilms International, publishers of <u>Dissertation Abstracts International</u> (copyright © 1968-1988 by University Microfilms International), and may not be reproduced without their prior permission. Doctoral and master's theses may be purchased from University Microfilms International, 300 North Zeeb Road, Ann Arbor, Michigan 48106 or borrowed through interlibrary loan from the institution where the author's work was completed.

Several handbooks published by the United States Tennis Association and the United States Professional Tennis Association on the administration of tennis programs are included. Other USTA and USPTA resources can be identified in the <u>USTA Tennis Publications</u> catalog which is listed in this bibliography (item no. 462). Titles published or distributed by the United States Tennis Association may be obtained from the Publications Department, United States Tennis Association, Center for Education and Recreational Tennis, 707 Alexander Road, Princeton, New Jersey 08540. Those published by the United States Professional Tennis Association may be obtained by writing to the Merchandise Department, USPTA, P.O. Box 7077, Wesley Chapel, Florida 34249.

1   Addie, Pauline Betz. Tennis for everyone, with official USLTA rules. Washington, DC: Acropolis Books, 1973. 119 p. LC 72-12392. ISBN 0-87491-149-4.

The author explains in simple, easy-to-understand language how to serve, volley, execute a forehand or backhand shot, and determine the strategy for singles or doubles. Sections on tournament temperament and conduct, sportsmanship, and training are included. Photographs. Diagrams.

2   Aguilar, M. Kay. "The influence of programmed instruction on the achievement of specific skills in tennis." Ed.D. Dissertation. Greeley, Colorado: University of Northern Colorado, 1973. 90 p. UMI Order No. 741596.

The primary purpose of this study was to investigate the plausibility of utilizing programmed instruction for the teaching of tennis skills. A secondary purpose was to examine the influence of motor ability and academic aptitude on the learning of tennis skills, and to explore interaction effects between treatment and academic aptitude, and treatment and motor ability.

3   Anderson, Andy. Tennis for your child. New York: Carlton, 1987. 64 p. ISBN 0-8062-2919-9.

Tennis parents are the target audience of this book. It provides an overview of the problems most likely to be encountered with young children learning the game. Answers to specific questions ranging from how early should a child begin taking lessons to what to talk about on the way home after a long day of practice on the courts are offered. Bibliography.

4   Anderson, David J., and Anderson, Robert M. The science of tennis. Tucson, Arizona: Racquet, 1982. 146 p. ISBN 0-9617528-0-7.

Designed to benefit beginners, experts, pros, and coaches, this book makes simple physical factors that determine success in tennis easily understood. Chapters cover the flight of the ball, player movement, geometry of strategy, psychology, and concentration. Diagrams.

5   Anderson, Jean Phyllis. "An electromyographic study of ballistic movement in the tennis forehand drive." Ph.D. Dissertation. Minneapolis, Minnesota: University of Minnesota, 1970. 141 p. UMI Order No. 718117.

The purpose of this study was to investigate the muscular activity in the tennis forehand drive to determine if the muscle action potential of selected muscles gives an indication of either ballistic movement or varying degrees of ballistic movement in highly skilled and in lesser skilled individuals. The data for this study was obtained from nine women subjects, three of whom were assigned to each of three skill levels.

6   Anderson, Margaret Peggy Boyd. "Muscle patterning in the overarm throw and tennis serve: an electromyographic and film study of skilled and less skilled performers." Madison, Wisconsin: University of Wisconsin, 1976. Ph.D. Dissertation. 228 p. UMI Order No. 7628137.

The objectives of this study were to determine spatial-temperal characteristics common among skilled and less skilled performers and to describe the characteristics common to both the tennis serve and the overarm throw when the two skills were performed by individuals judged to be skilled in both sport skills and by individuals skilled in just one of the two sport skills.

Anderson, Robert M.   see: Anderson, David J.

7   Annarino, Anthony. Tennis: individualized instructional program. Englewood Cliffs, New Jersey: Prentice-Hall, 1973. 72 p. LC 74-88309. ISBN 0-13-903328-9.

This individualized instructional workbook is designed for the reader to achieve a high degree of physical conditioning, to develop tennis skills, and to acquire an understanding of tennis strategy. It includes tests, behavioral objectives, individualized lesson plans, and written assignments.

Anthony, John   see: Nacinovich, Michael J.

8   Anthony, Julie, and Bollettieri, Nick. A winning combination. New York: Scribner's, 1980. 264 p. LC 80-18095. ISBN 0-684-16710-7.

    One of the nation's top teaching pros and a psychologist combine to provide information about the mental and physical health aspects of tennis. Conditioning, nutrition, equipment, practice, and sportsmanship are discussed. Contains coaching tips for young players and their parents. Photographs. Index. Bibliography.

9   Antonacci, Robert J., and Lockhart, Barbara D. Tennis for young champions. New York: McGraw-Hill, 1982. 185 p. LC 82-164. ISBN 0-07-002145-7.

    After a brief discussion of the game and its history, the authors go into step-by-step instruction on racket grips, footwork, and forehand and backhand strokes. The serve, volley, advanced strokes, doubles play, and strategy are covered. Drawings. Index. Juvenile reading level.

9A Applewhaite, Charles, and Moss, Bill. Tennis: the skills of the game. Marlborough, England: Crowood, 1987. 122 p. LC 87-11065. ISBN 0-946284-99-7.

    Two top British coaches talk about grips, basic strokes, spin, advanced strokes, tactics, fitness, and practice methods. The principles of hitting effective shots are discussed. Sequence photographs. Diagrams. Index. Bibliography. An approved Lawn Tennis Association (British) publication.

9B Applewhaite, Charles, and Poynder, Jane. The LTA guide to better tennis. London: Pan Books, 1986. 144 p. LC 87-15893. ISBN 0-330-29660-4.

    Recent theories and techniques associated with tennis are described and discussed in this manual. Chapters cover basic strokes, stroke variations, use of spin, match play strategy, and the importance of systematic practice routines. Photographs. Published in association with the Lawn Tennis Association (British).

Appel, Martin   see: Stolle, Fred

10 Armstrong, Wayne Jackson. "The effects of videotape instant visual feedback on learning specific gross motor skills in tennis." Ed.D. Dissertation. Hattiesburg, Mississippi: University of Southern Mississippi, 1971. 116 p. UMI Order No. 729058.

The purpose of this study was to determine if the addition of videotape instant feedback will have a significant influence on the learning of gross motor skills, rate of learning, and form in tennis when compared to a standard lecture-demonstration program. The Broer-Miller Tennis Test was used to evaluate each student's performance.

11 Ashe, Arthur. Arthur Ashe's tennis clinic. Norwalk, Connecticut: Golf Digest/Tennis; dist. by Simon and Schuster, 1981. 144 p. LC 80-84951. ISBN 0-914178-44-X.

Ashe and several of the world's top players illustrate their shots. Of particular interest are the sections which cover strategy, conditioning, serve, and the volley. Based on Tennis magazine's "Tennis Clinic" series. Drawings (color).

12 Ashe, Arthur, and Robinson, Louie, Jr. Getting started in tennis. New York: Atheneum, 1977. 102 p. LC 77-5199. ISBN 0-689-10826-5.

Strokes, footwork, court behavior, practicing, and rules are covered in this book. It is especially aimed at the young black tennis player. Photographs. Glossary. Juvenile reading level.

13   Assaiante, Paul, editor. Championship tennis by the experts, how to play championship tennis. West Point, New York: Leisure, 1981. 208 p. LC 80-83978. ISBN 0-918438-23-3.

A compilation of articles by well known players and coaches, the information in this book can provide the reader with a new direction for skill development or reinforce a previously introduced teaching point. Photographs.

14   Avery, Cathy Ann. "The establishment of norms for two selected tennis skills tests at North Texas State University." M.S. Thesis. Denton, Texas: North Texas State University, 1978. 132 p. UMI Order No. 1312093.

The purposes of this study were (1) to establish validity and reliability for a modified service test, (2) to determine male and female norms for the service test, and (3) to establish norms for the Kemp-Vincent Rally Test.

Bairstow, Jeffrey   see: Gonzales, Pancho
                           Lott, George

15   Baker, Eugene H. I want to be a tennis player. Chicago: Childrens Press, 1973. 31 p. LC 73-738. ISBN 0-516-01746-2.

Two children learn to play tennis and participate in a tournament. Illustrated. Juvenile reading level.

16   Ballard, Marie Elizabeth. "The development of a test for assessing ability to serve in tennis." M.S. Thesis. Carbondale, Illinois: Southern Illinois University, 1978. 100 p.

The purpose of this study was to construct a valid, reliable, objective, and practical test for the tennis serve. Secondary purposes included: to define good performance of the serve; to estimate the objectivity of the scoring; to estimate the objectivity of the ratings; to study the independence of selected measures; and to estimate the reliability of measures of accuracy and velocity.

17 Barker, Sue. Playing tennis. New York: Taplinger, 1979. 133 p. LC 79-66012. ISBN 0-8008-6323-2.

The author emphasizes tennis basics: defensive and offensive strokes; fitness and training; techniques, tactics, and psychology; and sportsmanship. Photographs. Drawings. Index.

18 Barnaby, Jack. Advantage tennis: racket work, tactics, and logic. Boston, Massachusetts: Allyn and Bacon, 1975. 237 p. LC 74-22246. ISBN 0-205-04686-X.

The author believes racket skills require more attention in the learning stages than do other elements of the game. Accordingly, racket movement is emphasized in this book. A chapter is devoted to skill tests, rewards, and drills. Each chapter concludes with a list of questions which can be used for written or oral testing. Photographs. Diagrams. Index.

19 Barnaby, John M. Ground strokes in match play: techniques, tempo, and winning tactics. New York: Doubleday, 1978. 152 p. LC 77-16897. ISBN 0-385-12705-7.

The author teaches groundstrokes in the context of actual playing conditions. Stroke analysis and techniques are based on the level of the player rather than on a predetermined model. Illustrated.

20 Barnaby, John M. Racket work: the key to tennis. Boston, Massachusetts: Allyn and Bacon, 1969. 250 p. LC 68-58540.

The emphasis in this book is on teaching techniques for use with beginners, intermediates, and competitive players. The author's philosophy that teaching correct racket skills is the most important and time-consuming aspect of learning tennis is presented. Chapters are divided accordingly: philosophy, technique, singles, doubles, and coaching. Unique topics covered in-depth are percentage tennis and halfcourt shots. Photographs. Diagrams. Index.

Barrett, John   see: Rosewall, Ken

21 Bartlett, Michael, and Gillen, Bob, editors. The tennis book. New York: Arbor House, 1981. 368 p. LC 81-67222. ISBN 0-87795-344-9.

Much of the material in this book deals with memorable tennis matches and the lives of famous players. There is, however, a collection of excerpted pieces from the instructional works of some tennis greats including Tilden, Budge, Kramer, Gonzales, and Laver.

22 Barton, Joel R., and Grice, William A. Tennis. 3rd edition. Boston: American, 1984. 118 p. ISBN 0-89641-147-8.

Descriptions of the fundamental skills and advanced techniques in tennis are presented in this book. Game strategy, practice drills, conditioning exercises, and an evaluation section with sample test questions and answers are included for teachers. Photographs. Diagrams. Glossary.

23 Bassett, Glenn, and Galanoy, Terry. Tennis: the Bassett system. Chicago: Contemporary Books, 1977. 106 p. LC 76-55670. ISBN 0-8092-7916-9.

The authors discuss their personal counting system used with the backswing, step, hit, and follow-through. Photographs. Glossary.

24 Beecher, Marjorie Tatum. "Relationships of forward hip rotation velocity, magnitude of forward hip rotation, and composite arm-shoulder strength to the flat tennis serve ball velocity." M.S. Thesis. Springfield, Massachusetts: Springfield College, 1977. 78 p.

The purpose of this study was to determine the relationship between the following variables: the velocity of forward hip rotation and the velocity of a served tennis ball as initiated by the flat service motion; the magnitude of forward hip rotation and ball velocity of the flat serve; and the composite static strength of the arm, wrist, and shoulder and ball velocity of the flat tennis serve.

Bender, Fred   see: Howorth, M. Beckett.

25 Benjamin, David A. *Competitive tennis: a guide for parents and young players.* New York: Lippincott and Crowell, 1979. 168 p. LC 79-11515. ISBN 0-397-01326-4.

The world of tennis at the collegiate level is described in this book. The process of developing young players into winners is analyzed. Part of the book deals with the 1978 NCAA Championships, the history of the tournament, and former champions. Photographs.

26 Benjamin, David A., editor. *The ITCA guide to coaching winning tennis.* Englewood Cliffs, New Jersey: Prentice Hall, 1989. 257 p. LC 88-31796. ISBN 0-1350-7955-1.

The purpose of this book is to make coaches aware of the responsibilities involved in teaching, promoting, maintaining, and conducting the game of tennis. Several prominent university coaches discuss a wide array of topics which include recruiting, training and conditioning, psychology of coaching, determining team line-ups, sportsmanship, and team promotional activities. Photographs. Diagrams. Index. Charts.

27 Blackburn, Lois H. <u>A handbook for planning and conducting tennis tournaments.</u> Revised edition. New York: United States Tennis Association, 1986. 95 p. LC 79-103974.

This book is a detailed guide to organizing elimination tournaments from initial planning stages to the post-tournament wrap-up from the viewpoint of committee responsibilities.

28 Blaskower, Pat, and Williams, Joanne. <u>Women's winning doubles.</u> Santa Barbara, California: Santa Barbara Press, 1985. 110 p. ISBN 0-915643-10-3.

This book is directed to the over-35-year-old woman who wants to improve her partnership performance, and the club and league player who wishes to excel in local competition. It is designed as a self-correcting handbook to develop both stroke production and a strategy of winning. Drawings.

29 Blundell, Noel Leslie. "An analysis of the visual/perceptual attributes of male and female tennis players of varying ability levels." Ed.D. Dissertation. Knoxville, Tennessee: University of Tennessee, 1982. 133 p. UMI Order No. 8225324.

This study was designed to investigate visual acuity, visual phoria, depth perception, peripheral vision, and coincidence anticipation of tennis players. The Bausch and Lomb Vision Tester, the Howard-Dolman device, and the Bassin Anticipation Timer were used to measure attributes. The Pearson product-moment correlation analysis was utilized to determine the relationship between and within the visual/perceptual measures.

30 Bodenmiller, Gary. <u>Drills for skills: a handbook for tennis players of all abilities.</u> New York: United States Tennis Association, 1980. 131 p.

The drills contained in this book are classified as offensive or defensive and arranged progressively according to degree of difficulty. Diagrams. Bibliography.

31 Bockus, H. William. <u>Checklist for better tennis.</u>
    Garden City, New York: Doubleday, 1973. 152 p. LC
    72-97268. ISBN 0-385-04612-X.

    Instruction is presented in two formats: first, as
    numbered explanatory paragraphs providing the
    fundamentals for each stroke and second, as checklists
    numbered for reference during play. Special chapters
    cover tactics, handicapping, and sportsmanship.
    Diagrams. Drawings.

    Bollettieri, Nick   see also: Anthony, Julie.

32 Bollettieri, Nick. <u>Nick Bollettieri's junior tennis.</u>
    New York: Simon and Schuster, 1984. 254 p. LC
    84-10618. ISBN 0-671-50840-7.

    The "Bollettieri System" of tennis instruction is
    presented in this book. The book is filled with
    photographs of hitting techniques. Includes a chapter
    on drills and an appendix on tennis nutrition.
    Diagrams. Index.

33 Bollettieri, Nick. <u>Tennis your way.</u> North Palm Beach,
    Florida: Athletic Institute, 1982. 158 p. LC
    82-73472. ISBN 0-87670-066-0.

    This book presents a series of lessons for different
    level players to correct, learn, or improve their game.
    Student dialogue is included in some chapters to
    reinforce the author's key ideas. Drawings.

34 Bolliger, A. <u>Get fit for tennis.</u> London: Pelham
    Books, 1982. 189 p. LC 82-670253. ISBN 0-7207-1350-1.

    The purpose of this book is to give tennis players of
    every age and playing ability the opportunity to play
    under the best mental and physical conditions, and to
    help trainers and sports doctors give advice to tennis
    players. Photographs. Index. Bibliography.

Learning Tennis

35 Boltin, Alan S. Bathroom tennis: 8 minutes a day to learn, improve and maintain your tennis game at home. New York: Ballantine Books, 1978. 54 p. LC 78-52212. ISBN 0-345-27619-1.

Despite its title, this book provides the reader with serious conditioning exercises and mind training programs which can be practiced anywhere. Photographs. Diagrams.

36 Borg, Bjorn. My guide to better tennis. London: Express Newspapers Ltd., 1981. 92 p. ISBN 0-85079-1189.

Through the use of photographs and cartoons, Borg introduces the reader to his personal ideas about tennis. Areas covered include the groundstrokes, principles of the serve, types of serve, returning serve, net play, the volley, and the smash. Juvenile reading level.

37 Borg, Bjorn. My life and game. New York: Simon and Schuster, 1980. 184 p. LC 80-17322. ISBN 0-671-41207-8.

The former number one player in the world illustrates and describes his groundstrokes, serve, return of serve, volley, spin, lob, training, and court philosophy. Photographs.

Bouchard, Paul   see also: Fogleman, Harry.

38 Bouchard, Paul. Tennis drills and skills illustrated. Minneapolis, Minnesota: Conrad, 1974. 130 p.

The drills and games in this book are for all levels of play. Each drill is clearly illustrated and described. The use of backboards, ball machines, and rebound nets are encouraged. Diagrams.

Bowden, Mary Carillo   see: Elstein, Rick

39 Brabenec, Josef. <u>Tennis: the decision making sport</u>.
    North Vancouver, British Columbia: Hancock House, 1980.
    144 p. LC C80-091150-4. ISBN 0-88839-052-1.

    This book deals with three major factors to consider
    when playing tennis: mental fitness, stroke technique,
    and physical fitness. Photographs. Diagrams.

    Brace, Reginald   see: King, Billie Jean.

40 Braden, Vic, and Bruns, Bill. <u>Teaching children tennis
    the Vic Braden way</u>. Boston: Little, Brown and Company,
    1980. 342 p. LC 80-20364. ISBN 0-316-105-12-0.

    The focus of this book is on parents who want to become
    involved with teaching their children important tennis
    fundamentals. The many aspects of how to actually teach
    the game to children are covered. The authors' approach
    is to have children strive to learn exactly the same
    stroking patterns as adults, though on a level consis-
    tent with their strength and coordination. Appropriate
    for teaching pros and coaches also.

41 Braden, Vic, and Bruns, Bill. <u>Vic Braden's quick fixes:
    expert cures for common tennis problems</u>. Boston:
    Little, Brown and Company, 1988. 135 p. LC 87-26099.
    ISBN 0-316-10514-7.

    This book is a "problems and cures" guide for helping
    players improve their game. Each problem is featured in
    a self-contained unit with its diagnosis, its cure, and
    accompanying photographs. Problems are introduced in the
    form of a player's statement, e.g., "I keep hitting the
    ball beyond the baseline." Chapters are divided
    according to the stroke analyzed. The strokes covered
    are the forehand, backhand, serve, return of serve,
    approach shot, volley, overhead, and lob.

42 Braden, Vic, and Bruns, Bill. <u>Vic Braden's tennis for the future</u>. Boston: Little, Brown and Company, 1977. 274 p. LC 77-5603. ISBN 0-316-10510-4.

A detailed book which emphasizes the loop backswing, the use of topspin, and the importance of understanding court design and angles. Contains material on how to develop confidence, how to perform well under pressures, and how to master a no-frills approach to strategy. Photographs. Diagrams.

43 Bradlee, Dick. <u>Instant tennis: a new approach based on the coordination, rhythm and timing of champions</u>. New York: Cornerstone Library, 1974. 128 p. LC 62-13467. ISBN 0-8159-5811-0.

The author presents a method of teaching beginners based on principles of motion economy. He advocates that the right foot should move foreward before hitting the forehand and backhand. Consequently, the player should not stand sideways to the net when hitting groundstrokes. His theory is based on the actual hitting methods of past champions and what he calls the ballistic swing. Photographs. Drawings.

44 Brecheen, Joel. <u>Count one! to top tennis technique</u>. Tucson, Arizona: Palo Verde, 1969. 111 p. LC 70-95603.

Intended for the student or teacher, this book presents the author's unique "beal method" of learning tennis. The main section includes six lessons on the strokes and the game itself. Includes coaching tips. Photographs. Diagrams.

45 Brent, R. Spencer. <u>Pattern play tennis</u>. Garden City, New York: Doubleday, 1974. 140 p. LC 72-89295. ISBN 0-385-05874-8.

The concept of "pattern play" teaching is presented in this book written for instructors. The premise is that tennis is a game of repetitive patterns and tennis teachers need to simulate these patterns for the student during instruction. The author believes the volley should be taught first to beginning students. Diagrams. Drawings.

46 Breskvar, Boris. Boris Becker's tennis: the making of a champion. Champaign, Illinois: Leisure, 1987. 128 p. ISBN 0-88011-290-5.

This book, written by Becker's coach, describes the techniques and teaching methods used at the Sports College in Leimen, Germany. The author emphasizes the importance of concentration on the progress of the individual player in terms of style and potential achievement. Topics covered include stroking techniques, the two-handed backhand, physical training, the psychology of training and competition, match preparation, tennis for older players, adapting to different kinds of court surfaces, and injury prevention. Photographs (color). Diagrams.

47 Brewer, Lewis. Professional tennis drills. New York: Scribner's, 1985. 192 p. LC 85-02066. ISBN 0-684-18298-X.

Seventy-five drills designed to help every player develop a winning game are contained in this book. Special features include drills for footwork, general technique, physical conditioning, and match play simulations. Published in cooperation with the United States Tennis Association. Illustrated.

48 Brody, Howard. Tennis science for tennis players. Philadelphia: University of Pennsylvania, 1987. 152 p. LC 86-30735. ISBN 0-8122-1238-X.

The laws of physics applied to the game of tennis are explained and analyzed in this book. Topics investigated include the shape of the racket, stringing patterns, ball spin, court surfaces, hitting angles, plotting game strategies, and reaction time. Photographs. Diagrams. Graphs. Index.

Brown, Jim   see also: Meinhardt, Tom

49 Brown, Jim. Tennis: strokes, strategy, and programs. Englewood Cliffs, New Jersey: Prentice-Hall, 1980. 294 p. LC 79-23982. ISBN 0-13-903351-3.

This is a book for teachers, coaches, parents, program directors, club professionals, and volunteer workers. The author succinctly covers tennis history and equipment, strokes, strategy, psychological factors, teaching, competitiveness, and practicing. Photographs. Drawings. Index. Bibliography. Glossary.

50 Brown, Jim. Tennis: teaching, coaching, and directing programs. Englewood Cliffs, New Jersey: Prentice-Hall, 1976. 192 p. LC 75-33047. ISBN 0-13-903344-0.

This book describes how to become a successful tennis coach and administrator. Tips from psychology, communication skills, and human growth and development are combined with the practical aspects of teaching tennis to help the reader design and supervise effective tennis programs. Photographs. Diagrams. Bibliography.

51 Brown Jim. Tennis without lessons. Englewood Cliffs, New Jersey: Prentice-Hall, 1977. 154 p. LC 76-18801. ISBN 0-13-903252-5.

The author believes it is possible to learn tennis without formal instruction by applying general principles of hitting strokes and developing a methodical approach to correcting errors. Photographs. Bibliography. Glossary.

52 Brown, Michael J. Tennis rules and techniques in pictures. New York: Putnam, 1987. 80 p. LC 87-2416. ISBN 0-399-51405-8.

This book illustrates the fundamental techniques necessary for the young beginning player to learn the game. Sections include footfaulting, playing with pace, and scoring, including the Van Alen Simplified Scoring System (VASSS). Drawings.

Bruns, Bill   see: Braden, Vic.

53 Bryant, James E. *Game, set, match...a beginning tennis guide.* Englewood, Colorado: Morton, 1986. 128 p. ISBN 0-89582-149-4.

This book is designed to serve as a reference guide for players actively receiving tennis instruction. Chapters, logically arranged, cover basic strokes, rules of play, strategy, drills, tennis psychology, and equipment. Photographs. Diagrams. Index. Glossary.

54 Bryant, James E. *Tennis: a guide for the developing tennis player.* Englewood, Colorado: Morton, 1984. 200 p. ISBN 0-89582-101-X.

Written for beginners and intermediate players, this book provides visual samples of strokes, strategy, and basic concepts. Index. Glossary. Illustrated.

55 Budge, John Donald. *Budge on tennis.* New York: Prentice-Hall, 1939. 180 p. LC 39-12276.

Following an opening biography of Budge by Allison Danzig, the former tennis great espouses his theory of winning tennis and proceeds to describe the fundamentals of stroking. Court psychology, strategy, and the game of doubles are also covered. Photographs.

56 Bunis, Alvin W., and Williams, Roger. *The tennis grand masters: how to play winning tennis in the prime of life.* Norwalk, Connecticut: Golf Digest/Tennis; dist. by Simon and Schuster, 1983. 161 p. LC 83-81075. ISBN 0-914178-53-9.

The experiences, techniques, and observations of the Grand Masters form the backbone of this book which addresses a select and rapidly growing segment of the world's tennis population. Photographs.

Bunker, Linda K.   see also: Rotella, Robert J.

57   Bunker, Linda K., and Rotella, Robert J. **Mind, set, and match: using your head to play better tennis.** Englewood Cliffs, New Jersey: Prentice-Hall, 1982. 173 p. LC 82-9113. ISBN 0-13-583484-8.

A technique of combining mental and physical training to achieve optimal performance is presented in this book. It explains how to set realistic goals and attain them, how to develop confidence and concentration, how to master relaxation techniques to help eliminate inappropriate muscle tension, and how to get the most out of your lessons and practice sessions. Drawings. Index.

58   Burkett, Donald. **Peaking through tennis: a mind/body guide to peak performances.** Champaign, Illinois: Water Park, 1979. 112 p. LC 79-90731. ISBN 0-935486-00-3.

This book looks at tennis as the sum of four interrelated elements or games: emotional, social, intellectual, and physical. The author believes full potential can be achieved by integrating these four parts of the game. The result is tennis "centering." Drawings.

Burleson, Clyde   see: Morton, Jason.

59   Burrus-Bammel, Lei Lane. "The volley method versus the ground strokes method of teaching beginning tennis." Salt Lake City, Utah: University of Utah, 1975. Ph.D. Dissertation. 92 p. UMI Order No. 7517853.

This study was designed to determine the effects of two beginning tennis teaching methods, the volley approach and the ground stroke approach, in college student's skill acquisition. Preliminary skills tests administered were the Revised Dyer Backboard Test and the Broer-Miller Forehand-Backhand Drive Test.

60   Burwash, Peter, and Tullius, John. Peter Burwash's tennis for life. New York: Times Books, 1981. 197 p. LC 80-50767. ISBN 0-8129-0952-6.

The author, founder of Peter Burwash International the world's first network of traveling tennis coaches, shares his understanding and unique teaching techniques. For professionals and coaches alike. Photographs. Diagrams.

Buxton, Angela   see: Jones, Clarence M.

61   Campbell, Kenneth Gordon. Playing tennis when it hurts. Millbrae, California: Celestial Arts, 1976. 109 p. LC 75-28753. ISBN 0-89087-155-8.

The author gives detailed instructions about how to play without aggravating an injury, how to prevent ailments from happening, how to overcome and heal injuries, and how to warm up properly before a match. Includes specific exercises to overcome common difficulties. Photographs. Glossary.

62   Campbell, Shep. Quick tips from the CBS tennis spot. Norwalk, Connecticut: Golf Digest/Tennis; dist. by Simon and Schuster, 1981. 188 p. LC 80-84952. ISBN 0-914178-45-8.

The purpose of this book is to help the reader raise the level of his play and get more fun out of the game. Each page makes a concise, graphic point that's easy to remember and can be applied immediately on the court. Selected from the 75-second "Tennis Spots" broadcasted on radio station WCBS-AM in New York City and the CBS Radio Network since 1973. Photographs.

63   Cantin, Eugene. Topspin to better tennis. Mountain View, California: World, 1977. 200 p. LC 77-73877. ISBN 0-89037-075-3.

The author emphasizes the use of topspin in competitive tennis. Photographs. Diagrams.

64 Capobianco, Ann M. "Relationships between success in selected situations in tennis and the outcome of competition." M.A. Thesis. Montclair, New Jersey: Montclair State University, 1978. 56 p.

This study evaluated the relationships between key points or situations in a tennis match and the final outcome of the match. It evaluated the relationships between: winning the fifth point in a game (when tied at 30-30) and winning the game; winning the seventh game in a set (when tied at 3-3) and winning the set; and winning the second set (creating a 1-1 tied situation) and winning the match.

Carillo, Mary   see: Elstein, Rick
                       Navratilova, Martina

65 Carrow, Richard Wells. "Teaching tennis with televised lessons: a comparative study of two teaching methods." Ed.D. Dissertation. Tempe, Arizona: Arizona State University, 1976. 87 p. UMI Order No. 7700352.

The purpose of this study was to determine the effect of teaching tennis with televised lessons which were combined with small group, teacher instruction. An experiment was designed to substitute televised lessons for the teaching functions of demonstration and class organization to allow the teacher to concentrate more time on the functions of interpretation of results and correction of errors.

66 Casewit, Curtis W. America's tennis book. New York: Scribner's, 1975. 214 p. LC 74-10714. ISBN 0-684-13900-6.

This is a beginning book on learning basic tennis strokes and terminology. Besides instruction, tennis careers, treatment of injuries, and tennis camp information are provided. Photographs. Bibliography. Glossary.

67 Cath, Stanley H.; Kahn, Alvin, and Cobb, Nathan. <u>Love and hate on the tennis court: how hidden emotions affect your game.</u> New York: Scribner's, 1977. 178 p. LC 77-476. ISBN 0-684-14925-7.

This book, written by two psychiatrists and a journalist, reveals the emotions that turn up on the tennis court and suggests ways to minimize their effects. The book includes case studies of the authors' patients who play tennis and are able to relate the game to other facets of their lives.

Chafin, M.B.   see: Moore, Claney.

68 Champion, Rick. <u>Yoga tennis: awareness through sports.</u> Phoenix, Arizona: A.S.I.A., 1973. 222 p. LC 73-85393. ISBN 0-914106-02-3.

Yoga is applied to teaching tennis in this book. Emphasis is placed on preparing a player spiritually and physically to participate in the sport. Includes breath control techniques, methods of relaxation, and exercises. Photographs.

Chapin, Kim   see: King, Billie Jean

Chappell, Annette Jo   see: Dickmeyer, Lowell.

69 Charles, Allegra. <u>How to win at ladies' doubles.</u> New York: Arco, 1975. 151 p. LC 75-3780. ISBN 0-688-03797-0.

Contains standard doubles instruction. The author places emphasis on the importance of playing side-by-side at the net. Photographs. Diagrams. Bibliography. Glossary.

70 Chase, Edward Tinsley. Covering the court. Garden City, New York: Doubleday, 1976. 63 p. LC 74-12679. ISBN 0-385-05502-1.

The author's premise is "the ability to cover the court is the most basic condition for winning in tennis." Chapters discuss pre-match preparation, fundamentals of match play, faking and spin, angles and depths, and court coverage in doubles. Diagrams. USTA Instructional Series.

71 Chavez, Rick, and Nieder, Lois Smith. Teaching tennis. Minneapolis, Minnesota: Burgess International Group, 1982. 144 p. LC 81-71259. ISBN 0-8087-4803-3.

The unique feature of this book is a chapter devoted to teaching objectives which are described and classified as cognitive, psychomotor, and affective. Also contains chapters on class organization, all levels of tennis instruction, strategy, evaluation, and coaching. Photographs. Diagrams. Index. Bibliography. Glossary.

72 Claxton, David Brannan. "A behavioral analysis of more and less successful high school tennis coaches." Ed.D. Dissertation. Tempe, Arizona: Arizona State University, 1985. 143 p. UMI Order No. 8601866.

The purposes of this study were to analyze and describe the coaching behaviors of more and less successful high school boys' tennis coaches from the Phoenix, Arizona area, to compare the findings of the more successful coaches to the less successful coaches, and to compare the behaviors of the tennis coaches with results of similar studies of coaches of team sports.

Cobb, Nathan   see: Cath, Stanley H.

73 Codiga, Michael A. "A study to determine the relationship of selected physiological variables and playing ability of male collegiate tennis players." M.S. Thesis. Provo, Utah: Brigham Young University, 1985. 43 p.

The purpose of this study was to identify the physiological characteristics important to tennis players and determine which one is most prominent in improving and predicting playing ability at an extremely high level such as intercollegiate tennis.

Cohen, Joel   see: Seixas, Vic

Collins, Bud   see also: Laver, Rod

74 Collins, Bud and Hollander, Zander, editors. <u>Bud Collins' modern encyclopedia of tennis.</u> New York: Doubleday, 1980. 389 p. LC 79-8919. ISBN 0-385-13093-7.

This book covers the sport of tennis on an international level. It includes rules, history, yearly summaries of significant events, and results of major tournaments since 1919. Contains biographical sketches of many of the world's greatest players. Photographs. Index. Glossary.

75 Collins, D. Ray; Hodges, Patrick B., and Haven, Betty H. <u>Tennis: a practical learning guide.</u> Bloomington, Indiana: Tichenor, 1985. 152 p. LC 86-140557. ISBN 0-89917-436-1.

This text is designed as a learning resource for all player levels. It uses high-speed photography to help describe the mechanics of various strokes. Includes a skills test for classifying students by ability level or for measuring student achievement. Drawings. Bibliography. Glossary.

76 Collins, Ed. <u>Watch the ball, bend your knees, that'll be $20 please!</u> Ottawa, Illinois: Green Hill, 1977. 216 p. LC 76-55626. ISBN 0-916054-50-0.

Learning Tennis

A compilation of dozens of newspaper tennis instructional columns, this book includes a table of contents by subject and recommended drills.

77 Complete guide to tennis. New York: New American Library, 1975. 386 p. LC 75-324003.

General instruction on grips, serve, techniques, strategy, rules, and strokes are included in this book. The Van Alen Simplified Scoring System (VASSS) is described. Photographs. Diagrams. Glossary.

78 Connolly, Maureen. Power tennis. New York: A.S. Barnes, 1954. 85 p. LC 54-9167.

"Lil Mo" illustrates the techniques and strategies which she used to become one of the all-time great women players. Includes chapters on how she learned to play the game and the importance tennis played in her life. Photographs. Diagrams. Index.

79 Connors, Jimmy, and LaMarche, Robert J. Jimmy Connors: how to play tougher tennis. Trumbull, Connecticut: Golf Digest/Tennis; dist. by Simon and Schuster, 1986. 188 p. LC 85-72331. ISBN 0-914178-78-4.

Text and full-color photography are blended in this book to capture the star's personality, inner drive, and powerful stroking technique.

Conroy, John   see: Haynes, Connie
                      Kraft, Eve

80 Coombs, Charles. Be a winner in tennis. New York: Morrow, 1975. 128 p. LC 74-23262. ISBN 0-688-22020-7.

The fundamental aspects of the sport of tennis are covered in this book including a brief history of the game, the layout of the court, grips, physical conditioning, techniques of the serve, ground strokes, and volley. The final chapter dramatizes the course of a set of singles from the viewpoint of one of the players. Photographs. Diagrams. Index. Glossary. Juvenile reading level.

81 Copley, Bruce Burley. "An anthropometric, somatotypological and physiological study of tennis players with special reference to the effects of training." Ph.D. Dissertation. South Africa: University of the Witwatersrand, 1980. UMI Order No. 0535309.

This study was conducted in order to present a comprehensive description and analysis of the morphological and physiological characteristics of professional and amateur team players.

82 Cormier, Steven Charles. "The effects of augmented visual cues on the performance of groundstroke consistency for beginning college-age tennis classes." M.S. Thesis. Tuscon, Arizona: University of Arizona, 1982. UMI Order No. 1319451.

The study compared the skill performance attained by university men and women in learning forehand and backhand groundstrokes in four beginning tennis classes under three different augmented visual feedback devices (rope; covered net; and a combination of the rope and covered net; plus a control group).

Couzens, Gerald Secor   see: Trabert, Tony

Cox, Mark   see also: Riessen, Clare

83 Cox, Mark. Lawn tennis: how to become a champion. London: William Luscombe, 1975. 123 p. LC 77-351916. ISBN 0-86002-023-1.

In addition to standard instruction, the author discusses the use of spin, the advantages and disadvantages

of the two-handed backhand, and doubles strategy.
Photographs. Diagrams.

84   Creek, F.N.S. Teach yourself lawn tennis. London:
     English Universities, 1968. 180 p. ISBN 0-340-05636-3.

     This book explains how to play tennis and gives detailed
     lessons of all the strokes and many of the tactics of
     the game. Photographs. Diagrams.

85   Crooke, John. Better tennis. Tadworth, Surrey: Kaye
     and Ward, 1984. 132 p. ISBN 0-7182-1465-X.

     The author's theme of Ball/Bat (racket)/Body/Brain runs
     throughout the book moving from elementary advice
     through to a comprehensive analysis of every aspect of a
     player's game. Photographs. Diagrams.

86   Cutler, Burt. So you think you know tennis. Los
     Angeles: Price/Stern/Sloan, 1977. 79 p. LC 77-9457.
     ISBN 0-8431-0427-9.

     This book contains a series of questions and answers on
     some of the fine points of tennis. Drawings.

87   Cutler, Merritt. Basic tennis illustrated. New York:
     Dover, 1980. 111 p. LC 80-65738. ISBN 0-486-24006-1.

     Essential stroke production and simple tactics are
     outlined in this book. Each stroke is briefly described
     and illustrated by the author. Separate sections cover
     women's tennis, mixed doubles, court surfaces, and
     weather conditions. Unabridged republication of the
     author's The tennis book (New York: McGraw Hill, 1967).
     Drawings.

88   Cutress, Bryan. Tennis. Morristown, New Jersey:
     Silver Burdett, 1980. 60 p. LC 80-50935. ISBN
     0-382-06425-9.

The thrill and suspense of competition tennis are captured in this book which reveals some of the top players' secrets on winning matches and illustrates fundamental techniques. Photographs. Index. Juvenile reading level.

89 Davidson, Owen. Tackle lawn tennis this way. London: Stanley Paul, 1970. 124 p. LC 79-27847. ISBN 0-09-103510-4.

The reader is taken step-by-step through the basics of tennis with the emphasis placed on the mechanics of the game. A chapter is devoted to successful courtcraft which can be the deciding factor in a match between two players of near equal ability. Photographs. Juvenile reading level.

90 Davis, Jim. The on court book of tennis drills. Peachtree City, Georgia: Davis Turner, 1986. 188 p. ISBN 0-961-4062-0-8.

Drills gathered from many sources including those of the author are arranged and illustrated for quick and easy recall in the book. The drills are arranged to allow tennis instructors to preselect drills which support specific instruction, e.g., groundstrokes, serve, volley, overhead, and lob. Game, agility conditioning, and exercise drills are also included. Diagrams (color). Index.

91 Davison-Lungley, Robin. Let's play tennis. London: Octopus Books, 1979. 96 p. ISBN 0-7064-1003-3.

The author provides an instructional guide for beginners and intermediates wishing to improve their game and technique. Chapters cover the basic strokes, the service, tactics and training, coaching, and etiquette. Photographs (color). Index. Glossary.

92 DeGroot, William L. Tennis and you. Englewood, Colorado: Morton, 1984. 105 p. ISBN 0-89582-124-9.

Learning Tennis 27

This book covers the basics of each stroke, discusses offensive and defensive strategies in singles and doubles, and offers mental and physical hints along with drills and exercises designed to improve one's game. Checklists to help players improve their performance are also included. Photographs. Glossary.

93 Deegan, Paul J. The basic strokes. Mankato, Minnesota: Creative Educational Society, 1976. 31 p. LC 75-41383. ISBN 0-87191-502-2.

Part of a series of books on tennis basics, this book describes and illustrates how to hit the forehand and backhand groundstrokes. Creative Education Sports Instructional Series, Volume I. Juvenile reading level.

94 Deegan, Paul J. Serving and returning service. Mankato, Minnesota: Creative Educational Society, 1976. 31 p. LC 75-31813. ISBN 0-87191-495-6.

Part of a series of books on tennis basics, this book describes and illustrates the serve and the return of serve. Creative Education Sports Instructional Series, Volume 2. Juvenile reading level.

95 Deegan, Paul J. Volleying and lobs. Mankato, Minnesota: Creative Educational Society, 1976. 31 p. LC 75-35614. ISBN 0-87191-496-4.

Part of a series of books on tennis basics, this book describes and illustrates how to hit the volley and lob. Also covered are the half-volley and overhead. Creative Education Sports Instructional Series, Volume 3. Juvenile reading level.

95A Deflassieux, Alain. Tennis. London: Hamilton Children's, 1986. 34 p. LC 86-18891. ISBN 0-24111-862-X.

Translated from the French, this book contains fundamental information about learning the game of tennis. Illustrated. Juvenile reading level.

95B Deflassieux, Alain. Tennis: basic techniques and tactics. London: Barrie and Jenkins, 1977. 91 p. LC 77-25139. ISBN 0-905703-02-2.

A basic instruction book which contains photographs and cartoon-type illustrations. Footwork, basic strokes, tactics, training, and equipment are covered. A trouble-shooting section discusses weather and varying court conditions. Glossary.

96 Devereux, Rick. Net results: the complete tennis handbook. Boston: Pathfinder, 1974. 182 p. LC 74-80452. ISBN 0-913390-07-0.

The fundamentals of tennis are covered in this book. One chapter is devoted to describing and analyzing a doubles match. Photographs. Diagrams. Glossary.

97 Dickmeyer, Lowell, and Chappell, Annette Jo. Tennis is for me. Minneapolis: Lerner, 1978. 46 p. LC 77-92300. ISBN 0-8225-1077-4.

Lessons on the forehand, backhand, and serve are found in this book. It progresses from the point of view of a child first learning tennis to competitive tennis. Sportsmanship is stressed. Photographs. Glossary. Juvenile reading level.

98 DiGennaro, Joseph. "The construction of forehand drive, backhand drive, and service tennis tests." Ed.D. Dissertation. New York: Columbia University, 1968. 136 p. UMI Order No. 698071.

The purpose of the study was to construct objective forehand drive, backhand drive, and service tennis tests for novice tennis players. These tests for accuracy in placement were based on: opinions of tennis authorities; recommended teaching progressions and methods of practicing the drives and serve; strengths and deficiencies in existing tennis skill tests; and the results of pilot projects relating to the nature of the tests.

Learning Tennis

DiGiacomo, Melchior   see: Scott, Eugene

99 Dintiman, George B., editor. Doctor tennis: a complete guide to conditioning and injury prevention for all ages. Richmond, Virginia: Champion Athletic, 1980. 96 p. LC 80-65623.

This book is designed to bring tennis players to their maximum level of conditioning. It offers suggestions for improving stroke power, court quickness, and sprinting speed. A prevention health program and diet are also included. Photographs. Index.

100 Doerner, Cynthia; Doerner, Peter, and Ozier, Dan. Winning tennis doubles. Chicago: Contemporary Books, 1978. 111 p. LC 77-91151. ISBN 0-8092-7697-6.

The author emphasizes the triangle concept - establishing a court position in which the partners are the side-by-side base with the ball the third point. Also covers mixed doubles and left-handers as partners and opponents. Photographs. Diagrams. Drawings.

Doerner, Peter   see: Doerner, Cynthia.

101 Douglas, Paul. The handbook of tennis. New York: Knopf, 1982. 280 p. LC 81-48125. ISBN 0-394-52373-3.

One of the most complete guides to tennis strokes, styles, and strategies, this book also includes sections on all-weather play, improving your attitude, and strength training. Photographs (color). Diagrams. Drawings. Index.

102 Douglass, Jack. Tennis. Dubuque, Iowa: Kendall/Hunt, 1977. 90 p. LC 77-152259. ISBN 0-8403-1709-3.

The purpose of this book is to assist instructors and students alike to develop their skills and knowledge of tennis. Coverage includes grips, footwork, basic and advanced strokes, spin, deception, and conditioning. Photographs. Lesson quizzes.

103 Driver, Helen Irene. Tennis for teachers. International edition. Madison, Wisconsin: Monona-Driver, 1964. 219 p. LC 64-24034. ISBN 0-910982-00-7.

A classic book on instruction in which the author provides tennis teachers with teaching philosophy and methodology for beginning players. The methods presented in this book represented the consensus of opinion among women coaches in the 1930s. Photographs. Diagrams. Index. Bibliography. Glossary.

104 Driver, Helen Irene. Tennis self-instructor. Madison, Wisconsin: Monona-Driver, 1971. 109 p.

This book emphasizes the same instructional points presented in the author's Tennis for teachers (item no. 103). The self-instruction handbook is designed for use by students to improve their strokes and strategy. Includes a question and answer section. Photographs. Diagrams. Drawings. Glossary.

105 Duggan, Moira, and Scott, Eugene L. The tennis catalog. New York: Macmillan, 1978. 256 p. LC 77-17866. ISBN 0-02-028350-4.

The purpose of this book is to provide information about equipment, clothing, tournaments, careers, camps, magazines, and commercially manufactured tennis products. Photographs. Index.

106 Duroska, Lud. Tennis for beginners. New York: Grosset and Dunlop, 1975. 90 p. LC 74-94. ISBN 0-448-11792-4.

Photographs make up the bulk of this book which shows proper grips, correct hitting techniques for groundstrokes, serve, approach shots, volleys, lobs, smashes, and doubles positioning. Each chapter contains sequence photographs, illustrations of incorrect hitting styles, and practice hints and reminders. Juvenile reading level.

107 Durr, Francoise. <u>Doubles strategy: a creative and psychological approach to tennis.</u> New York: David McKay, 1978. 112 p. LC 77-21194. ISBN 0-679-20350-8.

For advanced players, this book compares doubles and singles in terms of the effects of the alley, strategy, and tactics. The game is covered thoroughly. Diagrams.

108 Eddy, Ruth, and LeBar, John. <u>Learning tennis together.</u> West Point, New York: Leisure, 1982. 208 p. LC 81-86512. ISBN 0-88011-031-7.

This book presents an easily understood procedure by which two people can help each other learn to play singles or improve their playing together. Each chapter includes stroke definition, ball trajectory, racket mechanics, body mechanics, grips, and drills. Photographs. Diagrams. Drawings. Glossary.

109 Edwards, Larry Randolph. "A comparison of a computer method versus a traditional method of teaching beginning tennis." Ed.D. Dissertation. University, Mississippi: University of Mississippi, 1978. 103 p. UMI Order No. 7824043.

The purpose of this study was to determine the effectiveness of using computer feedback to supplement the oral feedback of a traditional instructional method. The study was designed to determine if one method was more effective than the other in teaching tennis skill and knowledge.

110 Eldred, Vince. <u>Tennis without mistakes.</u> New York: Putnam, 1975. 224 p. LC 74-16589. ISBN 0-399-11309-6.

Each chapter in this book begins with a list of common mistakes, discusses how to correct the errors, and concludes with a list of tips to avoid making the same errors over again. Standard strokes, psychology, tactics, footwork, practicing, and handicapping are among the topics discussed. Photographs. Diagrams. Index.

111 Elliott, Bruce, and Kilderry, Rob. The art and science of tennis. Philadelphia: Saunders College Publishing, 1983. 218 p. LC 82-61050. ISBN 0-03-062501-7.

Written for the player, coach, and teacher, this book offers a comprehensive evaluation of a player's game. Chapters cover stroke production, strategy, sports psychology, training, teaching, and player evaluation for improved performance. Photographs. Diagrams. Index. Bibliography. Glossary. Saunders Physical Activity Series.

111A Elstein, Rick, and Bowden, Mary Carillo. Rick Elstein's tennis kinetics with Martina Navratilova. New York: Simon and Schuster, 1985. 255 p. LC 85-8331. ISBN 0-671-55540-5.

Tennis kinetics and the basic elements and rhythms of the sport are described in this book. It provides the reader with a personal developmental program consisting of dozens of drills and exercises for different levels of play. Also includes a section on tactics and strategy. Photographs. Diagrams.

Emerson, Roy   see: Laver, Rod

112 Enberg, Mary Lou. "Assessing perception of object directionality in tennis." Ph.D. Dissertation. West Lafayette, Indiana: Purdue University, 1968. 179 p. UMI Order No. 6812547.

The purpose of the study was to develop an instrument which would aid in assessing an individual's perception of object directionality and to determine whether this perceptual skill was related to overall skill in the game environment. The means of varying the visual input was motion picture films. A tennis film test and the Witkin revision of the Gottschaldt Embedded Figures Test were administered to subjects.

113 Errington, Joseph. "Qualitative biomechanics and the tennis ground strokes." Revised. 1983. 11 p. ERIC Document No. ED 227091.

This tennis stroke analysis is based on the application of biomechanic principles and is designed to help those who play tennis only once or twice a week. Illustrated.

114 Fahy, Carol Ann. "Reactivity of efficacy evaluation and prediction on performance of women tennis players." Ph.D. Dissertation. Los Angeles: California School of Professional Psychology, 1986. 119 p. Order No. 8626132.

Seventy-one female intermediate tennis players participated in a study designed to investigate the reactivity of a task-specific efficacy evaluation measure, the reactivity of a prediction of performance measure, and the combined reactivity effects of both measures on performance.

115 Fannin, Jim, and Mullin, John. <u>Tennis and kids: the family connection.</u> Garden City, New York: Doubleday, 1979. 194 p. LC 78-22317. ISBN 0-385-14378-8.

The authors emphasize their concept of "Score" - self-discipline, concentration, optimism, relaxation, and enjoyment. Specific exercises are provided to develop Score's on and off the court.

116 Faulkner, Edwin J. and Weymuller, Frederick. <u>Ed Faulkner's tennis: how to play it, how to teach it.</u> New York: Dial, 1970. 294 p. LC 70-76967. ISBN 0-8037-2244-3.

The emphasis in this classic book is on individualized, self-paced instruction with lessons presented in order of difficulty. Sequence photographs are used heavily to illustrate proper and improper methods of stroke production. Many chapters conclude with beginner's drills, teaching hints, or troubleshooting charts. Also covers tactics for match play and strategy.

Fay, Marion   see: Winnett, Tom

117 Fish, Richard Alan. The anatomy and psychology of tennis. 2nd edition. London: Maybank, 1968. 121 p. LC 72-106953.

Mental fitness, physical fitness, and technique are discussed in this book. Emphasis is placed on the mental fitness aspects of tennis. Psychology, concentration, tactics, and analysis of player character are covered. Photographs. Diagrams.

Fishman, Lew   see: Talbert, Peter

118 Fiske, Loring. How to beat better tennis players. Garden City, New York: Doubleday, 1970. 296 p. LC 74-97660. ISBN 0-385-00346-3.

A book for the average player which provides hints on how to improve strokes and play better doubles. Separate chapters cover lefthanders, poaching, mixed doubles, and senior tennis. Diagrams. Index.

119 Fogleman, Harry, and Bouchard, Paul. Tennis for the coach, teacher, and player. Revised edition. Minneapolis, Minnesota: Conrad, 1976. 104 p.

This book covers footwork, groundstrokes, the serve, volley, overhead, lob, return of serve, and approach shot. Also contains tennis strategy and the author's favorite drills. Glossary. Illustrated.

120 Ford, Scott. <u>Design B: how to play tennis in the zone</u>. South Bend, Indiana: Icarus, 1984. 125 p. LC 84-04677. ISBN 0-89651-153-7.

An alternative to conventional tennis, the author says "don't watch the ball," and advocates changing your visual focus and the way you perceive your body on the tennis court. Index.

121 Forer, Bernard. <u>A new practical tennis book: strokes, strategy, and successful play</u>. New York: Vantage, 1974. 127 p. ISBN 0-533-00768-2.

The level of instruction in this book varies from beginner to advanced player. After discussing tennis fundamentals, the author covers more technical aspects of the game such as slice, top spin, playing the serve, and the geometry of tennis. A section on doubles play discusses poaching and the Australian formation. Diagrams. Drawings.

122 Fotre, Vincent. <u>Why you lose at tennis</u>. New York: Barnes and Noble, 1973. 103 p. LC 72-9913. ISBN 0-06-463326-8.

This book discusses why players lose and how they can increase their chances of winning. Chapters cover ways of adjusting to different types of players, how to handle pressure, percentage tennis, and playing on various court surfaces. Photographs. Diagrams.

123 Fox, Allen. <u>If I'm the better player, why can't I win</u>. Norwalk, Connecticut: Golf Digest/Tennis; dist. by Simon and Schuster, 1979. 156 p. LC 79-63332. ISBN 0-914178-28-8.

The author focuses on the psychology of competition. Top players are used as examples since they set the standards mentally as well as physically for successful tennis.

124 Fox, John, and Vasil, Elizabeth. When do we get to play, coach? Glassboro, New Jersey: Glassboro State College, 1976. 56 p.

This book illustrates tennis lead-up games and drills for students, teachers, and coaches. Chapters cover groundstrokes, serve, lobs, smashes, and drop shots, advanced drills, ball machine drills, and creative competition. Drawings.

125 Fraser, Neale. Successful tennis: from beginner to expert in forty lessons. North Hollywood, California: Wilshire, 1977. 80 p. ISBN 0-87980-324-X.

The techniques and strategy behind successful tennis are outlined in this book. It consists of 40 lessons which progress quickly from the basic strokes to more difficult shots and discusses tactics and the fine points of championship play. Photographs. Diagrams. Glossary.

126 Fratzke, Michael Julius. "A comparison of three different teaching aids on the improvement of the forehand and backhand strokes among intermediate tennis players." Ed.D. Dissertation. Commerce, Texas: East Texas State University, 1978. 94 p. UMI Order No. 7909652.

The purposes of this study were (1) to determine the differences among the Champion Board, the flat surface wall, and the Ball Boy Machine as tennis teaching aids, (2) to determine the best rotational order of presenting these teaching aids, and (3) to determine which teaching aids were effective tools for tennis skill improvement.

127 Frazier, Claude Albee, editor. The doctor's guide to better tennis and health. New York: Funk and Wagnalls, 1974. 126 p. LC 74-1281. ISBN 0-308-10105-7.

The physiological aspects of tennis are explored in detail in this book. The collection of essays written by medical doctors cover many topics including how to cope with minor injuries, taping and bandaging, bursitis, back strain, knee problems, plantaris, achilles, eye injuries, tennis elbow, sunburn, and allegies. Diagrams.

128 Frazier, Claude Albee, editor. Mastering the art of winning tennis: the psychology behind successful strategy. Toronto: Pagurian, 1974. 151 p. LC 74-79518. ISBN 0-919364-63-2.

This book is about how a player can prepare psychologically to win a match and stay "psyched up" to "psyche out" an opponent. Chapters written by prominent coaches and physicians cover gamesmanship, overcoming slumps, choking, mixed doubles, and stroke control. Photographs. Index. Bibliography.

129 Fuertges, Donat Robert. "The effect of programmed instruction on selected tennis skills, knowledge and attitudes." Ph.D. Dissertation. Salt Lake City, Utah: University of Utah, 1971. 123 p. UMI Order No. 7124495.

The general problem of this study was to determine differences, if any, between two instructional methods in achieving specific developmental aspects in tennis, among selected groups of college men and women.

Galanoy, Terry   see: Bassett, Glenn

130 Gallwey, W. Timothy. The inner game of tennis. New York: Random House, 1974. 141 p. LC 73-20582. ISBN 0-394-49154-8.

In this popular book the author explores the limitless potential within the human body through the medium of tennis. The author's thesis is that "neither mastery nor satisfaction can be found in the playing of any game without giving some attention to the neglected skills of the inner game--the game that takes place in the mind of the player."

131 Gallwey, W. Timothy. *Inner tennis: playing the game*. New York: Random House, 1976. 173 p. LC 76-14199. ISBN 0-394-40043-7.

A philosophical manual, the author applies his thesis described in *The inner game of tennis* (item no. 130) to real life situations. Mental and physical exercises to help people attain inner serenity are provided by using examples from the game of tennis. Emphasis is placed on the importance of concentration.

132 Gamble, Robert John. "Early environmental factors reported by amateur tennis players." Ph.D. Dissertation. Buffalo, New York: State University of New York, 1985. 151 p. UMI Order No. 8518751.

The purpose of this investigation was to gain insight into the significance of early tennis experiences for subsequent levels of tennis proficiency. The study examined the environmental influences of (1) age when first learning the game, (2) family support, and (3) initial learning experience.

133 Garner, Stan. *The Stan Garner tennis improvement method*. New York: Tactical Marketing, 1977.

Some of the author's points are to play with any grip that feels comfortable, two hands are better than one on the backhand, and the service toss is not as important as the arm's full extension. Diagrams. Drawings.

134 Gautschi, Marcel. *Tennis: playing, training, and winning*. New York: Arco, 1979. 144 p. LC 78-17159. ISBN 0-688-04692-9.

This book contains basic points written on the left side and discussion on the right side of each page. Includes a chart to assess one's own weaknesses, a list of exercises, and a chart to compile "third party" assessments of a player's achievement in competition. Diagrams. Drawings. Bibliography. Glossary.

Learning Tennis   39

135 Gebhardt, Deborah L., editor. "Instructors: are they
     significant?" 1976. 19 p. ERIC Document No. ED
     211494.

     This study focused on the effect of instructors and of
     using two different methods of teaching tennis on skill
     acquisition. Players received beginning instruction in
     either the traditional groundstroke (using a full grip)
     teaching method or the volley (using a graduated length
     grip) teaching method. All subjects were pre- and
     post-tested on the Broer-Miller Forehand-Backhand Drive
     Test.

136 Geist, Harold, and Martinez, Cecilia A. Tennis psychol-
     ogy. Chicago: Nelson-Hall, 1976. 127 p. LC 75-17651.
     ISBN 0-88229-120-3.

     This book applies simple psychological principles to
     tennis in the hope that people who play and watch the
     game will apply them successfully. The author believes
     the most important elements in the psychology of tennis
     are understanding yourself and the psychological assess-
     ment of your opponent. Photographs. Glossary.
     Cartoons.

137 Gensemer, Robert. Intermediate tennis. Englewood,
     Colorado: Morton, 1985. 216 p. ISBN 0-89582-130-3.

     The purpose of this book is to help experienced players
     who want to improve their game. It is divided into four
     sections: hitting the ball, strategy for singles and
     doubles, mental and physical preparation, and aerobic
     conditioning. Photographs. Diagrams. Index.
     Glossary.

138 Gensemer, Robert. Tennis. 3rd edition. Philadelphia:
     Saunders College Publishing, 1982. 102 p. LC 81-53084.
     ISBN 0-03-060106-1.

     This book is designed to offer something for tennis
     players of all levels. It covers the nature and purpose
     of tennis, needed equipment and its care, basic skills,
     rules and scoring, and game strategy. Drawings.

Bibliography. Glossary. Saunders Physical Activity Series.

Gillen, Bob   see also: Bartlett, Michael

139 Gillen, Bob, editor. <u>Winning tennis: strokes and strategies of the world's top pros</u>. Radnor, Pennsylvania: Chilton, 1978. 154 p. LC 77-26831. ISBN 0-8019-6648-5.

The articles which comprise this book appeared originally in <u>Tennis USA</u> magazine. Each stroke is discussed and followed by sequence photographs. Also covers tactics and techniques of singles and doubles play. Diagrams. Bibliography.

140 Givens, Billye Kay. "A philosophical analysis of the relationship between the whole-man concept and tennis." Ed.D. Dissertation. Stillwater, Oklahoma: Oklahoma State University, 1980. 85 p. UMI Order No. 8103300.

The author analyzed the relationship between the whole-man concept and tennis by finding evidence for the unity of man's nature and exploring the concept of integrated education as applied to physical education and tennis.

141 Godbey, Geoffrey, and Guadagnolo, Frank. <u>Triples: a new tennis game</u>. State College, Pennsylvania: Venture, 1980. 22 p.

According to the authors, triples has many advantages. It is a good way to learn tennis in physical education classes. It is a fast-paced game which involves more complex strategies and rapid exchanges. It is a team game introducing the aspects of teamwork, camaraderie, and psychologies of non-individual sports. Drawings.

Learning Tennis 41

142 Goffi, Carlos. <u>Tournament tough: a guide to junior championship tennis.</u> New York: Holt, Rinehart and Company, 1985. 144 p. LC 84-19741. ISBN 0-03-071598-9.

The author's unique program of winning is presented in this book. Subjects covered include how to pace a match, choking, anticipation, fitness and flexibility, and mental toughness. Each chapter contains a commentary by John McEnroe. Photographs. Glossary.

143 Gologor, Ethan. <u>Psychodynamic tennis: you, your opponent, and other obstacles to perfection.</u> New York: Morrow, 1979. 227 p. LC-78-31247. ISBN 0-688-03466-7.

Some long standing questions about the psychological aspects of tennis are addressed by the author. He believes if applied properly, psychology can improve a player's understanding of the game and his performance. Chapters are devoted to sports and shrinks, "psyching," masochism, risk-taking, and self-fulfilling prophecies. Index.

144 Gonzales, Pancho, and Bairstow, Jeffrey. <u>Tennis begins at 40: a guide for all players who don't have wrists of steel or a cannonball serve, don't always rush the net or have a devasting overhead but want to win.</u> New York: Dial, 1976. 180 p. LC 76-9416. ISBN 0-8037-5945-2.

The legendary author emphasizes physical fitness and the importance of practice. Not intended for competitive players. Photographs. Diagrams.

145 Gonzales, Pancho, and Hawk, Dick. <u>Tennis.</u> New York: Fleet, 1962. 123 p. LC 62-8027.

A book designed to be used on the court, this is a complete tennis manual written by one of the sport's great champions. Gonzales explains the correct grip and stroke for the forehand, backhand, serve, volley, half-volley, dropshot, and lob. Sections on singles strategy, practicing, and footwork are also included. Photographs. Diagrams. Drawings.

146 Gonzales, Pancho, and Hyams, Joe. <u>Winning tactics for weekend singles</u>. New York: Holt, Rinehart and Winston, 1974. 136 p. LC 74-4805. ISBN 0-03-013136-7.

This manual is designed in a question-and-answer format and presents information about the most asked about aspects of tennis. Chapters treat several topics including ground strokes, serving, net play, psychology and strategy, indoor/outdoor court surfaces, and tennis past the age of forty. Photographs.

147 Gonzales, Patricia Lea. "A comparison of the effectiveness of two serving motions in tennis." M.A. Thesis. Long Beach, California: California State University, 1973. 79 p. UMI Order No. 3565.

The purpose of this study was to compare the effectiveness of two different tennis serving motions in teaching beginning tennis to eleventh and twelfth grade girls enrolled in general physical education classes. One class was taught to serve with a no-backswing motion, and the other class was instructed in the full backswing motion. Hewitt's Speed of Service Test was administered to each group at the beginning and at the end of the instruction.

148 Gordon, Barbara. <u>Improving your tennis game</u>. New York: Hawthorn, 1973. 136 p. LC 73-9305. ISBN 0-8015-3978-1.

A series of articles originally published in <u>World Tennis</u> magazine, this book is presented as a dialogue between pupil and teacher. It is geared to common problems of intermediate players. Photographs. Diagrams. Drawings.

149 Gould, Dick. <u>Tennis, anyone?</u> 4th edition. Palo Alto, California: <u>Mayfield, 1985.</u> 100 p. LC 84-061923. ISBN 0-87484-720-6.

This is a book written by a successful international coach based on his own physical education classes for beginners through advanced players. Course methods and teacher-training programs are included. The techniques presented can be applied to group situations, community programs, and tennis camps. Photographs. Diagrams.

Graebner, Carol   see: Graebner, Clarke

150   Graebner, Clarke, and Graebner, Carol. Mixed doubles tennis. New York: McGraw-Hill, 1973. 107 p. LC 72-10043. ISBN 0-07-023879-0.

The game of mixed doubles is described and analyzed for the average player. Topics include stroke production, tactics, baseline strategy, fitness, and practice. The authors stress the importance of working together as a team. Diagrams. Drawings.

Gray, Howard C.   see: Sirota, Bud

151   Gray, Marvin R., editor. What research tells the coach about tennis. Washington, D.C.: Alliance For Health, Physical Education, and Recreation, 1974. 56 p. LC 74-21759.

This monograph provides a nontechnical presentation of the research findings relative to the competitive player. Areas studied include sociological, psychological, physical, and physiological characteristics of competitive players; mechanics of stroke production; and the organization and administration of tennis programs. Further research on tennis is recommended. Diagrams.

152   Greeley, Peg. Tennis charting: the graphic way. Saratoga, California: Magoos Umbrella, 1981. 16 p. ISBN 0-932904-02-5.

The author has devised a graphic-style charting system which permanently records the tennis stroke that decides each point in a match. What emerges are highly visible patterns showing how each match was won or lost, strengths and weaknesses of each player, the type of game each player plays, and how the match might have changed from set to set.

153 Greene, Robert Ford. <u>Tennis drills: on-and-off-court drills and exercises for beginners, intermediate players, and teaching professionals.</u> New York: Hawthorn, 1976. 233 p. LC 75-28689. ISBN 0-8015-7525-7.

Drills which can be performed by one or more players are described and illustrated in this book. Photographs. Diagrams. Glossary.

154 Greene, Robert Ford. <u>Tennis tactics: match play strategies that get immediate winning results.</u> New York: Putman, 1978. 149 p. LC 77-26216. ISBN 0-399-12120-X.

The author considers individual weaknesses and strengths in presenting tennis strategies. Discussion is limited to singles play. Photographs. Diagrams. Glossary.

Greer, Gordon   see: Talbert, William F.

155 Greer, Hugh Scott. "The teaching of classical versus functional techniques in the acquisition of a tennis skill." Ed.D. Dissertation. New York: Columbia University, 1969. 101 p. UMI Order No. 6916799.

This study was concerned with the technique used to teach beginners the forehand drive in tennis. The experimenter, through observation, study, and experience, prescribed what was labelled a functional technique which placed emphasis on different fundamentals when compared. The functional technique is based on principles of kinesiology and mechanics to produce a compact, consistent ballistic movement.

Grice, William A.   see: Barton, Joel R.

156 Groppel, Jack L. "A kinematic analysis of the tennis one-handed and two-handed backhand drives of highly-skilled female competitors." Ph.D. Dissertation. Tallahassee, Florida: Florida State University, 1978. 155 p. UMI Order No. 7917045.

This investigation was conducted to aid in the understanding of the mechanical differences between the one-handed and two-handed backhand drives and assist in the prediction of the optimal stroking method per individual.

157 Groppel, Jack L. Principles of tennis: techniques, drills, and strategies. Champaign, Illinois: Stipes, 1980. 105 p. LC 80-281461. ISBN 0-87563-187-8.

This book is for the individual who wants a short, yet complete description of stroke mechanics, drills, and strategies. The evolution of tennis and its origin in the United States are also included. Photographs. Bibliography. Glossary.

158 Groppel, Jack L. Tennis for advanced players and those who would like to be. Champaign, Illinois: Human Kinetics, 1984. 187 p. LC 83-83164. ISBN 0-93-125057-9.

The author applies the principles of biomechanics to analyze a player's efficiency of movement and determine how a player can perform more effectively. Bibliography. Index.

159 Groppel, Jack L., editor. "Proceedings of a national symposium on the racquet sports: an exploration of research implications and teaching strategies, June 13-16, 1979." Urbana, Illinois: University of Illinois, 1979. 325 p. ERIC Document No. ED 186373.

Hard scientific research and developments in teaching racquet sports were the focus of this conference. The psychological and sociological aspects of competition and participation in these sports with particular emphasis on the difference between males and females were covered in one section. Another section discussed physiology, sports medicine, biomechanics, motor learning and teaching strategies. Other topics treated in the proceedings included cinematic means, developing instructional aids, and a dynamic test for the comparison of rebound characteristics of three different brands of tennis balls.

160 Groppel, Jack L., and Sears, Ronald G., editors. "International symposium on the effective teaching of racquet sports. Proceedings, June 11-14, 1980." Urbana, Illinois: University of Illinois, 1980. 157 p. ERIC Document No. ED 209208.

The proceedings of this symposium cover various aspects of tennis. Teaching behaviors of university tennis instructors, successful methods of teaching serves and stroke techniques, sports psychology in tennis, and contemporary tennis research and its application by the practitioner were among the papers presented. Each paper is preceded by an abstract and many have a brief list of references.

161 Groppel, Jack L., and Shay, Arthur. Optimal tennis: the freeze-frame photographic approach to a better game. Chicago: Contemporary Books, 1983. 102 p. LC 83-1935. ISBN 0-8092-5602-9.

Basic strokes encountered when playing competitive tennis are covered in this book. The author combines the effectiveness of using models to demonstrate certain aspects of tennis with the performance techniques of professional tennis players during competition. Photographs. Index.

Guadagnolo, Frank   see: Godbey, Geoffrey

162 Hagerman, Betty Sue. "Effects of age and success on arousal levels of advanced female tennis competitors before and after tournament competition." M.Ed. Thesis. Austin, Texas: University of Texas, 1972. 120 p.

The purpose of this study was to investigate the effects of anticipation and participation in a competitive tennis match on arousal, as reflected by total body reaction time, within the different age and experience classifications of competitive female tennis players.

163 Hamer, Doris Ray. "The 'Mini-Match' as a measurement of the ability of beginning tennis players." P.E.D. Dissertation. Bloomington, Indiana: Indiana University, 1974. 71 p. UMI Order No. 7419592.

The problem of the study was to compare the use of the USTA's 7-out-of-12 tie-break system in a round-robin tournament to subjective ranking by judges as a determinator of playing ability for beginning women tennis players.

164 Harmon, Bob. *Use your head in doubles.* New York: Scribner's, 1979. 115 p. LC 78-31524. ISBN 0-684-16135-4.

Two dozen chapters of lucid explanations for the average player about various situations on the court and how to handle each make up the contents of this book. Diagrams.

165 Harmon, Bob, and Monroe, Keith. *Use your head in tennis.* Revised edition. New York: Crowell, 1974. 230 p. LC 74-10715. ISBN 0-690-00584-9.

This book is intended for the average player who wants advice on how to beat players on the same level. Strategy is emphasized. Diagrams.

166 Hatcher, Paul Graham. "An investigation of the interrelationships existing among psychological aggression,

court aggression and skill in male and female intercollegiate tennis players." Ph.D. Dissertation. Nashville, Tennessee: George Peabody College for Teachers of Vanderbilt University, 1979. 136 p. UMI Order No. 8016145.

The purpose of this study was to determine the relationship between court aggression under varying conditions of high and low chances of success; to ascertain the varying degrees of aggression exhibited by selected strokes; and to determine the extent to which psychological aggression was related to skill and court aggression and to determine its role in performance.

Haven, Betty H.   see: Collins, D. Ray

Hawk, Dick   see: Gonzales, Pancho

167 Haynes, Connie; Kraft, Eve, and Conroy, John. Speed, strength and stamina: conditioning for tennis. Garden City, New York: Doubleday, 1975. 94 p. LC 74-12691. ISBN 0-385-09758-1.

Detailed exercises, advice for keeping in shape, and a tennis diet are discussed in this book. Questions are answered about fatigue and glucose, salt and cramps, and emergency treatments of tennis injuries. Drawings. Bibliography. USTA Instructional Series.

168 Haynes, Connie, and Kraft, Steven. The tennis player's diet: a guide to better nutrition on and off the court. Garden City, New York: Doubleday, 1978. 131 p. LC 78-4791. ISBN 0-385-12631-X.

This book discusses the basics of good nutrition and provides information for players who want to enhance their match performance. It includes tips on what to eat before a match and how to calm a nervous stomach; how and why to avoid food additives; how and why to decrease sugar consumption and increase fiber in the diet. Drawings. Bibliography. USTA Instructional Series.

169 Heath, Kathleen Frances. "A study of sex role, sex differences, locus of control, and expectancy of success in tennis among college students." Ph.D. Dissertation. Eugene, Oregon: University of Oregon, 1982. 415 p. Order No. 8215304.

The focus of this study was on the analysis of sex differences with respect to expectancy of success, actual performance, accuracy of prediction, and attribution of performance in tennis skills against the theoretical background of sex roles and locus of control. College students in beginning classes were asked to estimate their scores on two tennis skill tests and make causal attributions about their actual performance.

170 Hedges, Martin. The concise dictionary of tennis. New York: Mayflower, 1978. 278 p. ISBN 0-86124-012-X.

This handbook contains brief biographies of past and present players, information about tennis associations, a comprehensive listing of tennis terms, and results of major championships including winners and runners-up. Photographs. Drawings. Bibliography.

171 Hegmann, II, Edward Henry. "The effect of videotape viewing training on learning tennis skills when utilizing videotape replay for feedback." Ed.D. Dissertation. Philadelphia: Temple University, 1973. 81 p. UMI Order No. 741795.

This study compared two types of videotape replay viewing procedures, one which included instructor feedback during videotape replay sessions and one that did not include instructor feedback, in order to determine their effect on learning tennis skills.

172 Heitmann, Helen M. "Operational procedures for implementing mastery learning in physical education." 1982. 6 p. ERIC Document No. ED 240057.

This report contains guidelines for creating and implementing mastery-based learning modules for individualized instruction in physical education. Each learning module contains four parts: statement of learning objectives; delivery system; transactions (practice); and terminal objectives (evaluation). Sample modules include: performing the forehand groundstroke in tennis and having students develop and perform a target game for eye-hand coordination.

Heldman, Gladys   see: Segura, Pancho

173 Hensley, Larry Duncan. "A factor analysis of selected tennis skill tests." Ed.D. Dissertation. Athens, Georgia: University of Georgia, 1979. 177 p. UMI Order No. 8001007.

A battery of 14 tennis skill tests was administered to 80 subjects enrolled in tennis classes at the University of Georgia in order to determine the factors underlying the tennis playing ability of beginning level tennis players.

174 Herzog, Billie Jean. Tennis handbook. 4th edition. Dubuque, Iowa: Kendall/Hunt, 1982. 113 p. LC 83-720. ISBN 0-8403-2828-1.

This book is designed as a handbook for students participating in a physical education class, a private instructional tennis class, or for the individual wishing to improve his own personal tennis skills. Each skill section provides a listing of common errors and how to correct them. Includes a crossword puzzle and quiz. Photographs. Diagrams. Index. Bibliography. Glossary.

175 Hester, Hortense. "The effect of teaching aids on the performance of a selected tennis serve." P.E.D. Dissertation. Bloomington, Indiana: Indiana University, 1972. 86 p. UMI Order No. 7233275.

This study was concerned with the effect of teaching aids on the performance of the tennis serve executed by beginning tennis players. A short tennis racket, a tennis ball, and a combination of a tennis ball and a short tennis racket were the teaching aids used. One group did not use a teaching aid.

Hill, D.L.   see: Johnson, M.L.

176 Hilliard, Sherry A. "The construction of a test to measure perceptual ability in tennis for college women." M.S. Thesis. Denton, Texas: North Texas State University, 1972. 63 p.

The purposes of this study were 1) to identify some of the factors involved in tennis perceptual ability, 2) to devise a test to measure these factors, and 3) to determine if this test has any predictive validity.

177 Hines, Henry, and Morgenstern, Carol. Quick tennis. New York: Dutton, 1977. 113 p. LC 77-3402. ISBN 0-525-04275-X.

The author emphasizes the importance of knowing how to run properly on the tennis court. Includes drills to sharpen player reflexes and get off to a fast start when running for a ball. Photographs.

Hodges, Patrick B.   see: Collins, D. Ray

Hoffman, Greg   see: King, Billie Jean

178 Hohm, Jindrick. Tennis, play to win the Czech way. Toronto: Sports Books, 1987. 336 p. C86-095080-8. ISBN 0-920-90502-1.

This book is intended for players, coaches, and parents involved with tennis training. Based on a detailed analysis of the game, the book explains the techniques and tactics of contemporary Czech tennis, the methodology of practice, and sports training of tennis players. Attention is paid to physical and psychological preparation. Group methods are described. Photographs. Diagrams. Bibliography.

179 Holland, Dorothy Provence. "The effects of forearm strength on lateral epicondylitis." M.A. Thesis. Terre Haute, Indiana: Indiana State University, 1977. 79 p.

The purpose of this study was to determine whether any significant difference existed between dominant forearm strength (specifically extensor-supinator and grip strength) of tennis players with lateral epicondylitis and the forearm strength of players without this condition.

Hollander, Zander   see: Collins, Bud

Hook, Jim   see: Trabert, Tony

180 Hope, Sherman Allen. "An analysis of service effectiveness in championship men's tennis." Ed.D. Dissertation. College Station, Texas: Texas A & M University, 1986. 158 p. UMI Order No. 8625471.

The purpose of this study was to analyze the serve in championship men's tennis. Fifty championship men's tennis matches were randomly selected from a number of tournaments throughout the state of Texas.

181 Hopkins, Paulette Wong. "A comparison of movement times between the open and the closed stance for the tennis forehand groundstroke." M.S. Thesis. State College, Pennsylvania: Pennsylvania State University, 1981. 56 p.

Movement time as a function of the open and closed stance for a wide forehand groundstroke was studied. Female members from the Penn State varsity tennis team participated in the study. Dekan Automatic Performance

Analyzers and photo cells were used to measure reaction time, and two movement times.

182 Hopman, Harry. Better tennis for boys and girls. New York: Dodd, Mead, and Company, 1972. 95 p. LC 76-165672. ISBN 0-396-06365-9.

In drawing upon his experience, the author has written a book for young people in which he discusses grips and strokes, tactics and strategy involving court position for singles and doubles, training and preparation, practice in the home, the use of a wall for practice, etiquette, footwork, and the benefits of tennis as a game for life. Photographs. Glossary. Juvenile reading level.

183 Hopman, Harry. Harry Hopman's winning tennis strategy. Indianapolis: Bobbs-Merrill, 1978. 129 p. LC 78-19185. ISBN 0-672-52530-5.

The author discusses esoteric aspects of the game such as prematch preparation and how to handle your opponent's chop shots. Diagrams. Also published as Lobbing into the sun (Indianapolis: Bobbs-Merrill, 1975).

184 Hovis, Ford, editor. Tennis for women. Garden City, New York: Doubleday, 1980. 256 p. LC 73-75416. ISBN 0-385-15826-2.

This book is comprised of chapters written by women tennis stars. Each chapter covers a specific stroke. Additional material is devoted to court strategy, doubles, and mixed doubles. Photographs.

185 Howorth, M. Beckett, and Bender, Fred. A doctor's answer to tennis elbow: how to cure it, how to prevent it. New York: Chelsea House, 1977. 94 p. LC 77-4145. ISBN 0-87754-052-7.

The author, an orthopedic specialist, has written a book entirely devoted to the painful affliction of tennis elbow with specific, easy-to-follow exercises for care and prevention. Includes a Vulnerability Test to determine how susceptible the reader is to tennis elbow. Drawings.

186 Huang, Bob, and Shay, Arthur. <u>Teaching your child tennis</u>. Chicago: Contemporary Books, 1979. 71 p. LC 78-57474. ISBN 0-8092-7546-5.

Following a general introduction, the author presents ten lessons for teaching basic skills to children. Includes tennis games. Photographs.

187 Hull, Gordon. <u>The six insidious traps of college tennis and how to avoid them!</u> Mineola, New York: Goodworth, 1979. 212 p. LC 78-78177.

The author warns against hasty or ill-considered choices of schools by college players. The book contains ten actual, true-life stories of players who have been caught in one of the six "insidious" traps of college tennis. The stories are based on the author's personal acquaintances with players, coaches, and parents.

188 Hultgren, Barbara. <u>Ball persons: a trainer's manual</u>. New York: United States Tennis Association, 1981. 31 p.

Step-by-step instructions on how to train ball persons efficiently and systematically are presented in this handbook. A reproducible section of pointers for use by ball persons is included. Illustrated.

188A Hume, Joyce. <u>Play better tennis: 50 star tips</u>. London: Pelham Books, 1986. 121 p. LC 86-4243. ISBN 0-7207-1683-7.

The author uses photographs (color) of players in action to analyze the classic shots and tactical skills used by the world's greatest players. Also warns against the common errors that occur when these techniques are attempted by less talented players. Includes tips on choosing proper equipment and hints on match preparation.

Learning Tennis 55

189 Hunt, Leslie. *Inside tennis for women.* Chicago: Contemporary Books, 1978. 126 p. LC 77-91157. ISBN 0-8092-7715-8.

The author's premise is that women play a different game than men. This book is designed to help the female player decide what style of game suits her best and teaches the basic strokes that go into her particular style, including ground strokes, volleys, serves, and smashes. Includes a section on limbering exercises. Photographs. Diagrams.

190 Huss, Sally Moore. *How to play power tennis with ease.* New York: Harcourt Brace Jovanovich, 1979. 95 p. LC 78-20569. ISBN 0-15-236836.

The author shows how players can add power to their groundstrokes, serve, and volley by using a specific backswing and follow-through. Drawings.

Hyams, Joe   see: Gonzales, Pancho
                   King, Billie Jean
                   Trabert, Tony

Intercollegiate Tennis Coaches Association
         see: Benjamin, David A.

191 Irvine, Cecil Victor. *The mechanics of lawn tennis.* Salisbury, Rhodesia: Mardon, 1968. 147 p. LC 75-303507.

This book explains the details of each stroke, describes a 12-week training schedule for junior players, analyzes the doubles game, and covers the psychology of match play. Photographs. Drawings.

Isaacs, Richard S.   see: Zweig, John

192 Jacobs, Helen Hull. *Beginners guide to winning tennis.* North Hollywood, California: Wilshire, 1976. 93 p. LC 61-12638. ISBN 0-87980-283-9.

Basic and advanced strokes are described in this book. The author also covers position play, the spin of the ball, proper timing methods, doubles, and strategy. Ten mini-lessons for juniors are included. Reprint of the author's *The young sportsman's guide to tennis* (New York: Thomas Nelson, 1961). Photographs. Diagrams. Index. Bibliography. Glossary.

193 Jacobs, Helen Hull. *Improve your tennis.* London: Methuen, 1936. 36 p. LC W36-37.

Jacobs describes the ten cardinal rules of the game which she found most important, e.g., "Never change a winning game; always change a losing game." The author also gives succinct advice on practice and strategy. Photographs.

194 Jacobs, Helen Hull. *Modern tennis.* Indianapolis, Indiana: Bobbs-Merrill, 1933. 220 p. LC 33-11453.

The author combines biographical narratives of her matches with instructional tips in this book. Instruction is presented in stages beginning with fundamentals and advancing to match play. Photographs. Glossary.

195 Jacobs, Helen Hull. *Tennis.* New York: A.S. Barnes, 1941. 77 p. LC 41-51747.

The author attempts to present the game of tennis in its simplest terms. Three major strokes are analyzed in depth: the forehand, the backhand, and the serve. Additional topics considered are court positioning, ball spin, strategy, and doubles. Photographs. Diagrams. Index.

196 Jaeger, Eloise M., and Leighton, Harry. Teaching of tennis for school and recreational programs. Minneapolis, Minnesota: Burgess, 1963. 142 p. LC 59-14566.

The authors have prepared this handbook to aid teachers in skill analysis, class procedures, organization, ideas for the use of facilities and equipment, and appraisal of skills and tennis knowledge. Emphasis is placed on teaching in secondary school programs. Photographs. Diagrams. Bibliography. Lesson plans. Test. Teaching objectives.

Janes, George   see: Kenfield, John F., Jr.

197 Johansen, Norman Bruhn. "A comparative study of the effectiveness of four methods of teaching tennis." Ed.D. Dissertation. Columbia, Missouri: Univerity of Missouri, 1970. 154 p. UMI Order No. 7020791.

This study proposed to determine the effectiveness of four methods of teaching tennis: face-to-face, two combinations of video tape and face-to-face, and video tape only, as measured by achievement scores of college sophomore males on tennis knowledge, the tennis serve, spced of the tennis serve, tennis backhand stroke, and the tennis forehand stroke. Mean achievement gain was obtained from the pre- and post-test scores on Hooks' Tennis Examination and Hewitt's Tennis Achievcment Test.

198 Johnson, Dewayne J.; Oliver, Robert A., and Shields, Sharon L. Tennis. Boston: American, 1979. 67 p. ISBN 0-89641-040-4.

Three major sections make up this book: "An Introduction to Tennis" covers history, learning objectives, basic rules, and tennis equipment; "Instruction for Beginners" discusses grips, stance, and basic strokes; "Techniques For Advanced Players" analyzes specialty shots, game strategy, and includes self-evaluation tests.

Johnson, H. Mardi   see: Zebas, Carole J.

199   Johnson, Joan D., and Xanthos, Paul J. *Tennis*. 5th edition. Dubuque, Iowa: William C. Brown, 1988. 176 p. LC 87-70262. ISBN 0-697-00363-9.

This book contains chapters on stroke production, conditioning, warm-up drills, strategy, and the graduated length method for learning groundstrokes, serve, and volley. Photographs. Diagrams. Index. Bibliography. Glossary. Physical Education Activities Series.

200   Johnson, M.L., and Hill, D.L. *Tennis*. 2nd edition. Topeka, Kansas: Jostens, 1983. 122 p. ISBN 0-88136-009-0.

Illustrations form the core of this book which describes the mechanics of stroking. Applicable to all levels from beginners to tournament players and coaches. A self-test and list of additional readings appear at the end of each chapter. Drawings.

201   Jones, Ann. *Tennis -- up to tournament standard*. Reprint. Wakefield, England: EP Publishing Limited, 1977. 119 p. LC 78-670011. ISBN 0-7158-0579-7.

Techniques, tactics, and training are methodically presented in this book. Each groundstroke and specialty shot is explained and illustrated. Grips, court position, and racket work are also covered.

202   Jones, Clarence M. *How to play tennis*. Secaucus, New Jersey: Chartwell Books, 1979. 61 p. LC 77-91899. ISBN 0-89009-192-7.

For the beginner or intermediate, this book provides practical instruction in the essentials of tennis. Grips, the service, groundstrokes, rallying, tactics, psychology, practicing, and match preparation are covered. Photographs. Diagrams. Index.

203 Jones, Clarence M. Improving your tennis: strokes and techniques. London: Faber and Faber, 1973. 132 p. LC 73-165611. ISBN 0-571-11097-1.

Technical chapters on the service, advanced strokes, refinement of play, net play, and tennis check points are geared for intermediate and advanced players. Tennis intangibles cover reasons for nervousness, winning attitudes, and total commitment. Drawings. Diagrams.

204 Jones, Clarence M. Match-winning tennis: tactics, temperament and training. London: Faber and Faber, 1971. 166 p. LC 79-589150. ISBN 0-571-09289-6.

The author's purpose is to provide the reader with suggestions and advice on how to become more tactically adept on the tennis court. Chapters discuss how to spot weaknesses in your opponent, finesse in singles play, defense against net play, return of serve, positioning in doubles, and personality factors. Diagrams.

205 Jones, Clarence M. Tennis: how to become a champion. London: Faber and Faber, 1970. 146 p. LC 68-106276. ISBN 0-571-04714-9.

The author covers the service, groundstrokes, volleying, and tactics in analyzing techniques of winning tennis in this book for advanced players. The book describes psychological and neuro-muscular processes involved in learning tennis, building confidence, practicing, and conquering the factors that inhibit success. A chapter is devoted to concentration. Photographs. Diagrams. Drawings.

206 Jones, Clarence M. Your book of tennis. London: Faber and Faber, 1970. 64 p. LC 77-523600. ISBN 0-571-08767-1.

The author takes the reader through the principal strokes and explains with the help of action photographs and diagrams exactly how they are produced and how the ball is controlled. Special advice on varying techniques for players shorter than the height of the net is provided. Juvenile reading level.

207 Jones, Clarence M., and Buxton, Angela. <u>Starting tennis</u>. Woodbury, New York: Barron's, 1977. 96 p. LC 76-50669. ISBN 0-8120-5151-3.

This book offers beginners innovative instruction at the most crucial time - as they begin to establish their tennis skills. Chapters cover how to play the game, stroke-making, serving, elementary tactical play, and practice programs. Photographs. Diagrams.

Jones, Ross   see: Stranberg, Bo

Kahn, Alvin   see: Cath, Stanley H.

Kahn, E.J., III   see: Loehr, James E.

208 Kahrs, Karol Anne. "The relationship of mental image to skill performance in tennis." Ph.D. Dissertation. Columbus, Ohio: Ohio State University, 1972. 151 p. UMI Order No. 7227036.

The primary purpose of this investigation was to determine the relationship between mental image and skill performance of the forehand drive of women students enrolled in beginning tennis classes. In addition, a comparison was made of mental image and skill performance to determine if they were the same or different.

209 Kelly, Julie, and Kirwan, Nancy. <u>The tennis league handbook</u>. Hinsdale, Illinois: Finn Hall Enterprises, 1975. 83 p.

This handbook deals with the planning, operation, and structure of tennis leagues. It contains step-by-step planning guides, draw schedules, and scoring methods. Includes suggested tennis ladder rules. Diagrams. Charts.

210 Kenfield, John F., Jr. Teaching and coaching tennis. 4th edition. Dubuque, Iowa: William C. Brown, 1982. 152 p. LC 75-35433. ISBN 0-697-07184-7.

This book is designed as an aid to tennis teachers. It is divided into three sections: correcting specific problems for each stroke, group teaching, and coaching. Photographs. Diagrams. Bibliography.

211 Kenfield, John F., Jr., and Janes, George. The volley and the half-volley: the attacking game. New York: Doubleday, 1978. 62 p. LC 76-56310. ISBN 0-385-12633-6.

The author describes how to capture the net and counter an opponent's passing shots. Includes drills. Diagrams. Bibliography. USTA Instructional Series.

Kilderry, Rob   see: Elliott, Bruce

212 King, Billie Jean, and Brace, Reginald. Play better tennis with Billie Jean King. London: Octopus Books, 1981. 137 p. ISBN 0-7064-1223-0.

This is a book for players who do not need to be introduced to the fundamentals, but who want to improve their standard of performance. Contains informative and clear diagrams of court positioning in singles and doubles. Photographs. Index.

213 King, Billie Jean, and Chapin, Kim. Tennis to win. New York: Harper and Row, 1970. 157 p. LC 70-95969. ISBN 0-06-012393-1.

King takes the reader from the fundamentals of the game to sophisticated aspects of modern strategy. Special attention is devoted to percentage tennis, playing the backcourt game, rushing the net, playing on different court surfaces, conditioning, and overcoming wind, sun, and heat. Diagrams. Drawings.

214 King, Billie Jean, and Hoffman, Greg. Tennis love: a parent's guide to the sport. New York: Macmillan, 1978. 164 p. LC 77-25864. ISBN 0-02-563210-8.

The parent-child-tennis triangle is discussed in this book. The primary emphasis is on how to help children obtain proper instruction, how to help them deal with competition, and how to help them get the most out of their involvement with tennis. Drawings.

215 King, Billie Jean, and Hyams, Joe. Billie Jean King's secrets of winning tennis. New York: Holt, Rinehart and Winston, 1974. 116 p. LC 74-5095. ISBN 0-03-013141-3.

The authors pose and answer dozens of questions on the most asked about topics in tennis. Subjects covered include ground strokes, the serve, return of serve, net play, lobs, overheads, doubles, mixed doubles, and strategy. One chapter is devoted to female-oriented questions. Photographs.

216 King, Billie Jean; Stolle, Fred, and Hoffman, Greg. How to play mixed doubles. New York: Simon and Schuster, 1980. 191 p. LC 80-10750. ISBN 0-671-24620-8.

This book is for mixed doubles players who want to derive the maximum possible pleasure from the game and who are willing to put forth some time and effort. It focuses on court strategy, playing tactics, and communication between partners.

Kirwan, Nancy   see: Kelly, Julie

Learning Tennis

217 Kleiman, Carol, and Stephens, Russell. *You can teach your child tennis: a 30 day guide to tennis readiness.* New York: Fawcett, 1979. 127 p. LC 79-114859. ISBN 0-445-04403-9.

A how-to-do-it guide, this book begins with a demonstration on hitting the ball with the palm of the hand. Photographs. Diagrams.

218 Klotz, Donald D. *Tennis, keep it simple.* Dubuque, Iowa: Championship Books, 1989. 64 p. LC 88-70751. ISBN 0-697-08483-3.

The basic philosophy underlying the author's "volley method" of teaching tennis is described in this book. Beginners start near the net and move progressively toward the baseline as the strokes are learned. Many of the sections in this book are edited articles which originally appeared in *World Tennis* magazine. Photographs. Drawings.

219 Koch, Barbara A. "The effect of utilizing shorty tennis rackets on beginning tennis achievement by college women." M.S. Thesis. Macomb, Illinois: Western Illinois University, 1971. 46 p.

The purpose of this study was to determine the effect of using the shorty racket in women's beginning tennis classes at Western Illinois University.

Kraft, Eve   see also: Haynes, Connie

220 Kraft, Eve. *The tennis workbook - unit one: for beginners and advanced beginners.* Revised edition. New York: United States Tennis Association, 1986. 64 p. LC 80-496-62. ISBN 0-938822-62-4.

This is a programmed learning guide for the beginning student and an instructional outline for the teacher. It contains periodic review skill tests and a discussion guide on rules of play. Photographs.

221 Kraft, Eve, and Conroy, John. <u>The tennis workbook - unit two: for intermediate and advanced players</u>. Revised edition. New York: Scholastic Coach, 1982. 72 p. ISBN 0-938822-43-8.

This workbook is a self-programmed course of study for the intermediate and advanced player, as well as a syllabus for teachers and coaches. It includes periodic review tests and a discussion guide on tournament terminology. Illustrated.

222 Kraft, Eve, and Conroy, John. <u>The tennis teacher's guide: group instruction and team coaching</u>. Revised edition. New York: United States Tennis Association, 1985. 96 p. LC 80-425985. ISBN 0-938822-51-9.

The authors describe effective techniques of class organization: lesson planning, group formations, utilization of limited facilities, and teacher preparation. Included is an outline for the varsity tennis coach. Photographs. Diagrams.

Kraft, Steven   see also: Haynes, Connie.

223 Kraft, Steven, editor. <u>Tennis drills for self-improvement</u>. New York: Doubleday, 1978. 82 p. LC 77-78516. ISBN 0-385-12632-8.

Drills for intermediate and advanced players are presented from the perspectives of ten coaches. Diagrams. USTA Instructional Series.

224 Kraft, Virginia. <u>Tennis instruction for fun and competition</u>. New York: Grosset and Dunlap, 1976. 176 p. LC 73-18527. ISBN 0-448-11698-7.

The author tells the story of an over thirty year old beginner who learns how to play competitive tennis in one summer. Provides encouragement for adult beginners. Photographs. Index. Glossary.

Kramer, Jack   see also: Robertson, Max

225 Kramer, Jack. How to win at tennis. New York: Prentice-Hall, 1949. 182 p. LC 49-8620.

The author believes champions are made by a superior inner strength that enables them to surmount physical, mental, and natural barriers. The purpose of this book is to point the way for players to become champions by presenting instruction in the basic fundamentals of stroking and court temperament. Photographs. Glossary.

226 Kramer, Jack, and Sheehan, Larry. How to play your best tennis all the time. New York: Atheneum, 1977. 178 p. LC 76-534. ISBN 0-689-10757-9.

This is a book for the intermediate and advanced player. The authors cover groundstrokes, serving, tactics, mental preparation, and how to compete against different opponents. Diagrams.

227 Kriese, Chuck. Total tennis training. Grand Rapids, Michigan: Masters, 1988. 209 p. LC 88-22100. ISBN 0-940219-24-X.

Coaches and players will find this book helpful in understanding the physical, mental, and emotional aspects of tennis. Detailed descriptions of training techniques and guidelines for mental and emotional development are presented. Information on anaerobic and aerobic training, strength and flexibility training, nutrition, stroke production, technical skill development, injury prevention, and game styles are covered. Also included are keys to developing strategy and team unity and suggestions for momentum management and goal setting. Photographs. Diagrams. Bibliography. Drills.

228 LaCoste, Jean Rene. LaCoste on tennis. New York: Morrow, 1928. 263 p. LC 28-20613.

The author describes his personal approach to mastering the technical and psychological aspects of tennis. The basic strokes are covered as well as placing spin on the ball, match play temperament, and advice for beginners. LaCoste refers to many of his contemporaries' styles of play while discussing the mechanics of stroking. Photographs.

229 LaLance, Richard E. "A comparison of a self-directed learning approach to a traditional instructional approach in beginning tennis." D.A. Dissertation. Murfreesboro, Tennessee: Middle Tennessee State University, 1975. 134 p. UMI Order No. 7610249.

The purposes of this study were: (1) to compare a self-directed learning approach to teaching tennis to a traditional instructional approach and (2) to analyze and interpret the results of this comparison. Subjects were assigned to either the experimental group or the control group according to their total scores on Form A of Hewitt's Comprehensive Tennis Knowledge Test and Hewitt's Tennis Achievement Test.

LaMarche, Robert J.   see also: Conners, Jimmy

230 LaMarche, Robert J. *Tennis basics*. Englewood Cliffs, New Jersey: Prentice-Hall, 1983. 48 p. LC 82-21542. ISBN 0-13-903237-1.

The author presents the forehand, backhand, volley, and serve in an easy instructional style. A book for beginners. Illustrated. Juvenile reading level.

231 LaMarche, Robert J., editor. *Instant tennis lessons*. Norwalk, Connecticut: Golf Digest/Tennis; dist. by Simon and Schuster, 1978. 191 p. LC 77-92905. ISBN 0-914178-18-0.

In this book each page contains a tennis "tip" by a member of the United States Professional Tennis Association. Illustrations are included for each tip.

Learning Tennis 67

232 LaMarche, Robert J., editor. More instant tennis lessons. Norwalk, Connecticut: Golf Digest/Tennis; dist. by Simon and Schuster, 1984. 147 p. LC 84-80549. ISBN 0-914178-70-9.

A supplement to the author's Instant tennis lessons (item no. 231), this book contains 110 fully illustrated attention grabbing tips from some of the finest teaching pros in the game.

233 LaMarche, Robert J., editor. Teach yourself tennis. Norwalk, Connecticut: Golf Digest/Tennis; dist. by Simon and Schuster, 1980. 183 p. LC 80-66688. ISBN 0-914178-39-3.

This book is comprised of a series of articles from the "Instructional Portfolio" of Tennis magazine. Beginners can use it to get started in tennis and progress steadily with each chapter. Advanced players can use the book as a refresher course and to develop new strokes and strategies. Photographs. Diagrams.

Lajoie, Gesele   see: Lajoie, Robert.

234 Lajoie, Robert and Lajoie, Gesele. Tennis handbook and curriculum guide. North Vancouver, British Columbia: Hancock House, 1980. 47 p. LC C80-091140-7. ISBN 0-88839-043-2.

This handbook presents ideas on the teaching of tennis by way of objectives, program content teaching methods, sample lesson plans, and evaluation. It emphasizes the psychomotor aspects of skill development. Drawings. Physical Education Series.

235 Lappin, Greg. Tennis doubles: winning strategies for all levels. Edina, Minnesota: K.G. Books, 1985. 137 p. LC 84-081014. ISBN 0-930425-00-6.

This book is written in a programmed learning format and based on the author's "rhythm method" of tennis. Includes specific practice drills and positive self-rating cues. Catch phrases and jingles are used throughout the book for easy memorization of concepts. Each chapter contains a section which lists specific drills to practice shots and techniques on the court. Photographs. Diagrams.

236 Lardner, Rex. *The complete guide to tennis.* New York: Cornerstone Library, 1979. 126 p.

The author explains the rules of the game, describes proper clothing and equipment, and tells how and when to execute the basic strokes. Also included are chapters on tactics, doubles play, conditioning, practicing, and how to prepare for a match. Drawings. Glossary. Reprint of the author's *The complete beginner's guide to tennis* (Garden City, New York: Doubleday, 1967).

237 Lardner, Rex. *Finding and exploiting your opponent's weaknesses.* Garden City, New York: Doubleday, 1978. 80 p. LC 74-12730. ISBN 0-385-9103-6.

The author advocates an attacking game in this book. Attacking shots are described in detail, e.g., volley, smash, and serve. Drawings. USTA Instructional Series.

238 Lardner, Rex. *Tactics in women's singles, doubles, and mixed doubles.* Garden City, New York: Doubleday, 1975. 135 p. LC 74-12731. ISBN 0-385-09044-7.

This is a book for women tennis players which contains specific suggestions for exploiting opponents' weaknesses. Topics covered include playing with and against left-handers, pressuring opponents, receiving serve, the Australian doubles formation, and mixed doubles. Diagrams. Drawings. USTA Instructional Series.

239 Larson, Charles Leroy, Jr. "The effect of selected tennis racket and string variables on ball velocity and the force of ball-racket impact." P.E.D. Dissertation. Bloomington, Indiana: Indiana University. 120 p. UMI Order No. 8003466.

This study was conducted to determine the effect of tennis racket composition, racket flexibility, string type, and string tension on the force transferred from a tennis racket-tennis ball impact through the handle and the ball velocity following ball-racket impact.

240 Laver, Rod. <u>Tennis tips</u>. Chicago: Follett, 1977. 80 p. LC 76-50752. ISBN 0-695-80716-1.

Tips for beginners, intermediates, and advanced players are presented in this book. The table of contents can be used to find tips associated with a particular stroke or shot. Drawings.

241 Laver, Rod, and Collins, Bud. <u>The education of a tennis player</u>. New York: Simon and Schuster, 1971. 318 p. LC 70-139639. ISBN 0-671-20902-7.

Laver presents the reader with a personal narrative of his Grand Slam year (1969). Instructional tips are combined with descriptions of his major tennis matches during the year. Photographs. Index.

242 Laver, Rod, and Collins, Bud, editors. <u>Rod Laver's tennis digest</u>. Chicago: Follett, 1973. 288 p. LC 72-97511. ISBN 0-695-80387-5.

This is a compilation of articles from <u>World Tennis</u> magazine written by several authors covering a variety of topics ranging from instruction, styles of play, personalities, tactics, and strategy. The book begins with a series of mini-lessons from Laver. Photographs. Drawings.

243 Laver, Rod, and Collins, Bud, editors. <u>Rod Laver's tennis digest</u>, 2nd edition. Chicago: Follett, 1975. 288 p. LC 75-311253. ISBN 0-695-80527-4.

This edition supplements an earlier volume with the same title. It includes a beginners' key to tennis terminology intended to help readers understand tennis newspaper stories and fans listening to tennis commentary on television. Photographs. Diagrams. Drawings.

244 Laver, Rod; Emerson, Roy, and Tarshis, Barry. Tennis for the bloody fun of it. New York: Quadrangle, 1976. 158 p. LC 75-11479. ISBN 0-8129-0590-3.

This book provides information about basic and advanced shots, spins, tactics, concentration, doubles strategy, practice drills, and conditioning. It is particularly useful to left-handed players since there are many photographs of Laver demonstrating strokes.

245 Laver, Rod, and Pollard, Jack. How to play championship tennis. New York: Macmillan, 1965. 148 p. LC 64-18193.

Laver reminisces about his Grand Slam of 1962 and his early childhood tennis education before providing the reader, in prose style, with numerous tips on the fundamentals of stroking, the doubles game, and tactics. Photographs.

246 Laver, Rod, and Pollard, Jack. How to play winning tennis. London: Mayflower, 1970. 127 p. LC 72-589947. ISBN 0-583-19609-8.

Laver's hitting techniques and training methods are presented in a personal narrative format. Topics covered include getting the ball into play, the mental approach to a good backhand, the fundamentals of good volleying, the basics of an efficient forehand, techniques for successful doubles, and tactics. Photographs. Drawings.

Lawn Tennis Association (British)   see: Applewhaite, Charles

247 <u>Learning to play better tennis.</u> London: Collins, 1974. 61 p. ISBN 0-00-103311-5.

This book contains chapters on preparing to play, stroke production, improving play, and court tactics. Diagrams. Drawings (color). Test. Juvenile reading level.

248 Leary, Don J. <u>The teaching tennis pro.</u> Los Angeles: Pinnacle Books, 1979. 218 p. ISBN 0-523-40574-X.

This is a collection of teaching tips which originally appeared as newspaper columns. Each tip includes an illustration. Chapters are devoted to forehand, backhand, the serve and overhead, volleys and net play, conditioning, tactics, strategy, and mental preparation. Glossary.

LeBar, John   see: Eddy, Ruth

249 Lee, Frieda. "A study of sex differences in locus of control, tennis expectancy for success, and tennis achievement." Ph.D. Dissertation. Eugene, Oregon: University of Oregon, 1976. 78 p. UMI Order No. 7713202.

The purpose of this study was threefold: (1) to determine whether sex differences existed in locus of control and expectancy of success; (2) to determine the effects of class membership on expectancy of success and skill performance; and (3) to determine the degree of relationship between locus of control and a physical skill achievement such as tennis.

250 Leedy, Jack J., and Malkin, Mort. <u>Psyching up for tennis.</u> New York: Basic Books, 1977. 178 p. LC 76-43467. ISBN 0-465-06518-X.

The authors describe in depth and with humor the interrelationships between the mental and physical stresses and strains of tennis players in their pursuit of excellence. It makes players aware of the various physical functions involved in each mental and physical act of playing tennis. Index.

Leighton, Harry   see also: Jaeger, Eloise M.

251 Leighton, Harry. Junior tennis. New York: Sterling, 1974. 128 p. LC 73-93589. ISBN 0-8069-4072-7.

A lengthy chapter devoted to preparatory drills and exercises followed by chapters covering the forehand, backhand, and serve make up this book for beginners. Also includes sections on rules, scoring, etiquette, and basic strategy. Photographs. Index. Glossary. Juvenile reading level.

252 Leighton, Jim. Inside tennis: techniques of winning. North Hollywood, California: Wilshire, 1977. 192 p. LC 69-14432. ISBN 0-87980-340-1.

This book describes the development of a tennis player from beginner to a finished player. It is written for all types of tennis teachers and all player levels. It is based on the thesis that tennis is most effectively learned on levels of play (beginner, intermediate, and advanced), in logical steps of progression. Photographs. Index.

Lendl, Ivan   see also: Scott, Eugene

253 Lendl, Ivan. Hitting hot: Ivan Lendl's 14-day tennis clinic. New York: Random House, 1986. 108 p. LC 86-03277. ISBN 0-394-55407-8.

Strong groundstrokes and serves, sharp volleying, and thoughtful tennis strategy are emphasized in this book. For the advanced player. Photographs.

254 Lenglen, Suzanne. Lawn tennis: the game of nations. London: George G. Harrap, 1925. 127 p. LC 25-17043.

The author provides classic instruction for groundstrokes, volleys, overhead smashes, speciality shots, singles and doubles tactics, mixed doubles, and footwork. Photographs. Diagrams.

255 Lenglen, Suzanne, and Morris, Margaret. Tennis by simple exercises. London: William Heinemann, 1937. 195 p. LC 37-19290.

Lenglen describes how to hit the forehand and backhand drives, the volley, and the serve. The second part of the book contains preparatory exercises specifically designed for tennis by Morris. Photographs. Drawings.

256 Lenz, Bill. Unisex tennis. Port Washington, New York: Kennikat, 1977. 260 p. LC 76-7981. ISBN 0-8046-9147-9.

The author contends there are differences between men and women learning the game of tennis. He explains his theories as they apply to the physical, mental, and emotional differences between male and female players, the specific learning needs of each, and the basic strokes. Photographs. Diagrams.

257 Levisohn, Steven R., and Simon, Harvey B. Tennis medic: conditioning, sports medicine and total fitness for every player. St. Louis, Missouri: Mosby, 1984. 226 p. LC 84-14910. ISBN 0-8016-4669-3.

This book is divided into three sections: training for stamina, speed, power, and flexibility; common tennis pains and injuries and their recognition and treatment; and how tennis can fit into a program of good nutrition and sensible exercise for optimal health. Drawings. Index.

Lewis, Morey. see: Yale, Virginia.

258 Lindquist, Edith L. "Study of the cognitive plan in the acquisition of complex motor skill. Continuation of study I: good motor learners. Final Report." San Jose, California: San Jose State College, 1971. 226 p. ERIC Document No. ED 051523.

This study investigates a general organizational plan used by good motor learners in acquiring a complex motor skill (tennis serve). The General Serve Problem Solving Model (GSPS) was utilized. Subjects learned to serve by observing a loop film and still pictures and by asking questions.

259 Lisk, John Walter. "Effects of velocity, surface, and angle of incidence on angle of rebound of tennis balls." Ph.D. Dissertation. College Station, Texas: Texas A & M University, 1980. 212 p. UMI Order No. 8108025.

The purpose of this study was to determine and compare the effects of velocity, surface, and angle of incidence on angle of rebound and velocity of rebound of tennis balls.

260 Litz, David. A photographic guide to tennis fundamentals. New York: Arco, 1978. 110 p. LC 77-1533. ISBN 0-668-04185-4.

This book uses detailed sequence photographs to illustrate the different strokes and tactics of tennis. Glossary.

Lockhart, Barbara D.   see: Antonacci, Robert J.

261 Loehr, James E. Mental toughness training for sports. Lexington, Massachusetts: Stephen Greene, 1986. 191 p. LC 85-27199. ISBN 0-8289-0574-6.

The author tells how to achieve optimum performance by getting into the proper frame of mind. For the serious competitor. Bibliography. Illustrated.

Learning Tennis 75

262 Loehr, James E., and Kahn, E.J, III. Net results: training the tennis parent for competition. Lexington, Massachusetts: Stephen Greene, 1987. 154 p. LC 87-7583. ISBN 0-8289-0634-3.

The competitive aspects of junior tennis are analyzed in this book. The authors describe how parents can successfully introduce tennis to their children; how a child's competitive instincts may be developed and encouraged; how to curb temper tantrums, control choking, and eliminate tanking; how parents can help a coach, and how they can hurt; and how to avoid burning out the junior player. Photographs.

263 Loehr, James E., and Kahn, E.J., III. The parent-player tennis training program. New York: Stephen Greene, 1989. 165 p. ISBN 0-8289-0670-X.

This book shows how to relieve the stress and pressure that can make playing tennis much less enjoyable than it should be for children. Through a system of team building, parent profiling, written agreements, stress management and mental toughness training, parents are brought to a new level of understanding and personal effectiveness with their tennis playing children. The program consists of seven one-hour team training sessions. A companion volume to Net results: training the tennis parent for competition (item no. 262). Photographs. Questionnaire. Goals.

264 Loomis, James C. The tennis doctor: everything you always wanted to know about tennis but didn't know whom to ask. New York: Vantage, 1983. 240 p. LC 82-90673. ISBN 0-533-05582-2.

This book contains chapters on training and conditioning, tennis injuries, jogging, and how to correct problems with a player's game. Illustrates correct and incorrect stroking techniques to enable the reader to pinpoint flaws in stroking. Photographs. Glossary.

265 Lord, Sterling. Returning the serve intelligently. Garden City, New York: Doubleday, 1976. 60 p. LC 73-20532. ISBN 0-385-05297-9.

This book covers how to return serve in the deuce court, ad court, in singles, in doubles, and on different types of surfaces. It also includes how players can reduce errors, minimize the server's advantage, and launch their own attack. Drawings. USTA Instructional Series.

266 Lott, George, and Bairstow, Jeffrey. How to play winning doubles. New York: Simon and Schuster, 1979. 144 p. LC 77-92904. ISBN 0-914178-20-2.

The authors discuss all aspects of doubles. The effect of different court surfaces is covered in detail. Diagrams.

267 Loughlin, William Thomas. "The role of augmented knowledge of performance in the form of movement process correction in the acquisition of a motor skill." Ph.D. Dissertation. New York: New York University, 1980. 141 p. UMI Order No. 8110668.

The purpose of this study was to determine if augmented feedback, in the form of movement process corrections (MPC), facilitated the acquisition of a target/projectile task (the tennis forehand drive) because of its function as "information" or "reinforcement."

268 Loveless, Ada Letitia. "The utilization of mental practice in the learning of selected tennis skills." Ph.D. Dissertation. East Lansing, Michigan: Michigan State University, 1977. 206 p. UMI Order No. 7725257.

The purpose of this study was to investigate the effects of mental practice as a method to facilitate physical skill learning. The skills were the tennis forehand and service. Skill was measured in two ways: on performance and on form.

269 Lowe, Jack. Winning with percentage tennis: an expert's guide to smart court strategy. 3rd edition. North Hollywood, California: Wilshire, 1975. 92 p. LC 74-176273. ISBN 0-87980-327-4.

This book is designed to help the beginner and intermediate player understand the basic principles of how to play tennis. It is divided into two parts: "Stroke Production" which emphasizes the inside-out swing for groundstrokes, and "Court Strategy" which identifies the percentage shot in different playing situations. Diagrams.

270 Lumiere, Cornel, editor. The book of tennis: how to play the game. New York: Grosset and Dunlap, 1965. 92 p. LC 64-21266. ISBN 0-448-01948-5.

This book, compiled by the editors of World Tennis magazine, analyzes the "why" and "how" of playing correct tennis. Unique chapters cover elementary rallying and how to use a backboard in practice. Photographs. Drawings. Glossary.

271 Lumpkin, Angela. A guide to the literature of tennis. Westport, Connecticut: Greenwood, 1985. 235 p. LC 85-9941. ISBN 0-313-24492-8.

This work is a comprehensive guide to books, journals, and audiovisual materials covering the spectrum of tennis subjects. Chapters cover history, rules and administration, equipment, general and specific tennis techniques, health and fitness, psychological aspects of tennis, biographies, children's books, humor, films, and other publication formats. Index.

272 Lumpkin, Angela. Women's tennis: a historical documentary of the players and their game. Troy, New York: Whitston, 1981. 193 p. LC 79-57328. ISBN 0-87875-189-0.

The history of women's tennis from 1874-1978 is traced in this book. The careers of American and some non-American players which influenced the changing styles of play are analyzed. Photographs. Bibliographic references.

273 Luszki, Walter A. <u>Psych yourself to better tennis</u>.
North Hollywood, California: Wilshire, 1973. 146 p.
ISBN 0-87980-246-4.

The author examines the cerebral nuances of the game --
the tricks, the shortcuts, the art of concentration, and
the value of self-analysis. The book also covers
"sadistic" and "masochistic" tendencies in tennis, how
to reduce hostility in an opponent, and introduces
Freudian concepts to the tennis court. Photographs.

274 Luszki, Walter A. <u>Winning tennis through mental toughness</u>. New York: Everest House, 1982. 95 p. LC 81-19537. ISBN 0-89696-150-8.

The aim of this book is to help develop the three
crucial characteristics of mental toughness: determina-
tion, concentration, and confidence. It also includes
ideas on psychological preparation for match play, how
to capture momentum, the importance of knowing your
opponent's strengths and weaknesses, gamesmanship and
psychological warfare, and how to use behavior modification to improve your game. Photographs.

Lutz, Bob   see: Smith, Stan

275 Mabbitt, Terry. <u>Tennis</u>. Glasgow: Collins, 1979. 125 p. ISBN 0-00-411611-9.

The author's aim in this book is to show how all the
members of the family (from age four upwards) can learn
to play and enjoy tennis. Chapters cover ball sense,
the groundstrokes, the serve and volley, speciality
shots, tactics, left-handers, court manners, and more.
Photographs (color). Diagrams. Glossary.

Mabry, Clarence   see: Newcombe, John

276 MacBeth, Jon Lowell. "The effect of continuous and interval step training on attitudes, cardiovascular fitness, and tennis skills of beginning tennis students." Ed.D. Dissertation. Nashville, Tennessee: George Peabody College for Teachers, 1973. 88 p. UMI Order No. 7332617.

The purpose of this study was to compare the effects of two step training programs, one a continuous and the other an interval step training program, upon attitudes toward physical education, cardiovascular fitness, and tennis skills of beginning tennis players.

277 McCormick, Bill. Tennis. New York: Watts, 1973. 66 p. LC 73-3407. ISBN 0-531-00803-7.

This book discusses the origins of tennis, the game's equipment, rules, scoring, and plays. Also includes a brief description of some tennis greats. Illustrated. Juvenile reading level.

278 McCullough, Jeffrey F. Two-handed tennis: how to play a winner's game. New York: M. Evans, 1984. 176 p. LC 83-20759. ISBN 0-87131-425-8.

Ihe author presents techniques for hitting an array of two-handed shots in match play situations. Covers flat, topspin, and slice groundstrokes, grips, footwork, backswings, and volleying tactics. Photographs.

279 MacCurdy, Doug, and Tully, Shawn. Sports Illustrated tennis: strokes for success. New York: New American Library, 1988. 158 p. LC 87-32379. ISBN 0-452-26103-1.

This book covers the basic strokes in detail, specialty shots, tactics, psychology, practice methods, and positive thinking. Photographs. Drawings. Reprint, with updated photographs, of Sports Illustrated tennis (New York: Lippincott and Crowell, 1980).

280 McDonald, Kaye. "A comparison of the personality traits of participants and nonparticipants in high school interscholastic tennis programs for girls." Ed.D. Dissertation. Tempe, Arizona: Arizona State University, 1970. 81 p. UMI Order No. 713678.

The purpose of this study was to investigate the personality trait differences between high school girls who did or did not participate in interscholastic tennis. The instrument administered was Cattrell's High School Personality Questionnaire. Two random samples of 370 girls were drawn from lists provided by school districts and served as the nonparticipant samples. There were 145 freshman tennis participants, 83 nonteam members, and 116 varsity tennis participants in the other groups.

281 McLaughlin, Thomas Michael. "Load sharing in the forearm muscles prior to impact in tennis backhand strokes." Ph.D. Dissertation. Urbana-Champaign, Illinois: University of Illinois, 1978. 236 p. UMI Order No. 7821012.

This investigation determined the force distribution in the forearm muscles prior to impact during two types of tennis backhand strokes as performed by a professional tennis player. Two trials each of the subject's normal as well as simulated beginner, or "leading elbow," backhand strokes were selected for detailed analysis.

282 McPhee, John. *Levels of the game.* New York: Farrar, Straus, and Giroux, 1969. 150 p. LC 76-87219. ISBN 0-374-18568-9.

This is an in-depth study of a match between Arthur Ashe and Clark Graebner played at the U.S. Open in 1968. The sociological analysis attempts to show how early events in each player's life lead to the type of tennis style each played.

283 McPherson, Sue Lynn. "The development of children's expertise in tennis: knowledge structure and sport

performance." Ph.D. Dissertation. Baton Rouge, Louisiana: Louisiana State University, 1987. 193 p. UMI Order No. 8728205.

This research examined children's development of knowledge structure and sport performance in tennis. A knowledge test was designed to measure declarative knowledge and a serve and groundstroke skill test were developed to measure skill. An observational instrument was designed to record the components of performance for the serve and game play following the serve. Expert and novice players within two age levels, 10-11 year's old and 12-13 year's old were compared.

284 Malec, Luzanna A. "Anaerobic and aerobic capacity of selected Southern California female collegiate skilled and unskilled tennis players." M.S. Thesis. Fullerton, California: California State University, 1982. 52 p. UMI Order No. 1318573.

The aerobic and anaerobic capacity of ten skilled and ten unskilled collegiate female tennis players were compared in this study. Open circuit method of gas analysis during a graded exercise test, and the Margaria-Kalamen Power Test were used to measure the various physiological parameters.

Malkin, Mort   see: Leedy, Jack J.

285 Marcal, Haroldo. "Simplification of TNT (Talent-N-Timing) test for college students." Ph.D. Dissertation. Toledo, Ohio: University of Toledo, 1982. 56 p. UMI Order No. 8227815.

The purpose of this study was to develop a simplification of the TNT test to solve the problem of test administration to large college classes. The data for this investigation were obtained from 20 advanced tennis players, both male and female. The ability level of each subject was determined according to the TNT test scores.

286 Marcovicci, Jena. <u>The dance of tennis</u>. Richmond, Massachusetts: Dance of Tennis, 1986. 153 p.

This book is intended to provide the reader with a self-paced, relaxing method of enjoying the game and increase playing ability by showing how to let go of trying too hard. Music and dance are used to find natural inner rhythms of movement and deep levels of concentration. Photographs. Drawings. Bibliography.

Martinez, Cecilia A.   see: Geist, Harold.

287 Mason, R. Elaine; Walts, Kenneth; and Mott, Mary L. <u>Tennis</u>. Boston: Allyn and Bacon, 1974. 146 p. LC 73-84851. ISBN 0-205-03844-1.

Techniques that may be adapted to all ages and abilities of players are presented in this book. Chapters cover all strokes, footwork, etiquette, strategy, advanced skills, conditioning, and practice. The Graduated Length Method (GLM) is emphasized. Photographs. Diagrams. Bibliography.

288 Masuda, Kinzo. "Tennis backhand strokes: a comparative study between the two-handed backhand stroke and the one-handed backhand stroke for beginning tennis players." M.S. Thesis. Provo, Utah: Brigham Young University, 1978. 44 p.

The purpose of this study was to determine whether or not there is a difference in performance between the two-handed backhand stroke and the one-handed backhand stroke for men and women beginning tennis players.

289 Mead, Shepherd. <u>How to succeed in tennis without really trying: the easy tennismanship way to do all the things no tennis pro can teach you</u>. New York: McKay, 1977. 181 p. LC 77-1522. ISBN 0-679-50749-3.

This light-hearted book is intended to improve the success rate of its readers both on and off the tennis court. Chapters offer tips on club tennis, how to win in doubles, training, psychology, and social tennis. Index. Glossary.

290 Medlycott, James. *Tennis*. London: Macmillan, 1975. 89 p. LC 76-354443. ISBN 0-333-18385-1.

This book provides a practical step-by-step guide for readers interested in learning how to play tennis. An analysis of the qualities necessary to produce a champion is presented. Photographs (color). Drawings. Index. Glossary.

291 Meinhardt, Tom, and Brown, Jim, editors. *Tennis group instruction II*. Reston, Virginia: American Alliance for Health, Physical Education, Recreation, and Dance, 1984. 64 p. ISBN 0-88314-263-5.

A companion volume to the USTA's *USTA schools program tennis curriculum* (item no. 454), this manual is designed to assist physical educators and recreational leaders in effectively teaching tennis to beginner groups. Its primary concern is with those teachers who have little or no personal skill in the game. Topics cover stroke mechanics, teaching techniques and aids, and the safety and health of players. Photographs. Diagrams. Bibliography. Lesson plans. A publication of the National Association for Sport and Physical Education.

Merrihew, S. Wallis   see: Paret, J. Parmly

291A Messick, Jo Ann. "Prelongitudinal screening of hypothesized developmental sequences for the tennis serve and the effect of sex, experience, and age on developmental level." Ed.D. Dissertation. Greensboro, North Carolina: University of North Carolina, 1987. 262 p. UMI Order No. 8816352.

A cross-sectional test of the broad criteria of "stability" and "intransitivity" as proposed in motor stage theory was conducted to screen hypothesized developmental sequences within six body components of overhead serving in tennis. The effects of sex, experience, and age on the hypothesized developmental skill level of males and females in tennis serving were examined.

292 Metzler, Paul. Advanced tennis. Revised edition. New York: Sterling, 1972. 191 p. LC 68-18790. ISBN 0-8069-4000-X.

Written for the advanced player, this book presents clear explanations of common mistakes and demonstrates how to avoid them. Explains how to exploit strong points, how to reduce mental and physical errors, and how to overcome weaknesses. A chapter is devoted to temperament. Photographs. Diagrams. Drawings. Index.

293 Metzler, Paul. Fine points of tennis. New York: Sterling, 1978. 208 p. LC 77-93309. ISBN 0-8069-4199-7.

Intricate techniques and subtle aspects of the game are covered in this book. A section on temperament includes advice on how to deal with anger and self-pity during competitive play. For advanced players. Diagrams. Index.

294 Metzler, Paul. Getting started in tennis. New York: Sterling, 1972. 128 p. LC 70-180467. ISBN 0-8069-4050-6.

The author gives clear point-by-point explanations of the fundamentals of tennis. Points covered include how to watch the ball, how to keep long racket contact, proper forehand and backhand techniques, when to use topspin, and how to smooth out a swing. Photographs. Diagrams. Drawings. Index. Juvenile reading level.

295 Metzler, Paul. Tennis doubles: tactics and formations. New York: Cornerstone Library, 1976. 160 p. LC 74-31695. ISBN 0-346-12207-4.

In this book the author shows correct court positions for any situation. Basic strokes and formations to general tactics for serving and receiving are covered. Also included are suggestions on when to go to the net, how to play with a weaker partner, and how to lob aggressively. Photographs. Diagrams. Index.

296 Metzler, Paul. <u>Tennis weaknesses and remedies.</u> New York: Sterling, 1974. 96 p. LC 73-83459. ISBN 0-8069-4060-3.

The author encourages experimentation rather than following rigid rules in developing personal hitting techniques. Instruction emphasizes analyzing weaknesses and finding the proper remedy. Chapters cover grips, ground strokes, serving, volleying, ball spin, tactics, doubles, and left-hander weaknesses. Diagrams. Drawings. Index.

297 Michulka, Nony R. "The resilient effects of three string tensions in seven different tennis rackets." M.S. Thesis. Denton, Texas: North Texas State University, 1976. 57 p. UMI Order No. 1308941.

This study investigated the resilient effects of selected string tensions in the following rackets: Wilson T-2000, Head Professional, Head Master, Dunlop Fort, Dunlop Austral, and Yamaha Composite. The testing involved dropping a tennis ball 100 inches onto the racket face, which was stationary, and measuring the height of the ball bounce.

298 Miller, Susan Wilhelmy. "Achievement in tennis skills as related to different scheduling patterns." M.S. Thesis. Fullerton, California: California State College, 1972. 67 p. UMI Order No. 3251.

A school on flexible scheduling and a school on traditional scheduling were compared for instructional time differences and for skill achievement in tennis. Elective classes of sophomores, juniors and seniors were tested at the beginning of a tennis unit and again after five weeks of instruction.

Monroe, Keith   see: Harmon, Bob.

299 Monsaas, Judith Ann. "Talent development: a study of the development of world class tennis players." Ph.D. Dissertation. Chicago: University of Chicago, 1985.

The purpose of this study was to investigate the ways in which individuals reach the highest levels of accomplishments. Eighteen world-class U.S. men and women tennis players who had world rankings between 1968 and 1979 and their parents constituted the sample. Interviews were conducted to identify what parents, teachers and others did to encourage and promote their extreme talent development.

300 Montgomery, Jim. <u>Tennis for the mature adult</u>. Jackson, Mississippi: Hunter's Mountain Tennis Corporation, 1979. 113 p. LC 80-102046.

This book is for adults who want to learn tennis to improve their health by becoming more active physically. Emphasis is placed on motivation, physical precautions, a fitness program, and basic instruction. Bibliography.

301 Moore, Claney, and Chafin, M.B. <u>Tennis everyone</u>. 3rd edition. Winston-Salem, North Carolina: Hunter Textbooks, 1986. 243 p. LC 87-100285. ISBN 0-89459-213-0.

Equipment, scoring, principles of stroking, footwork, strategy, conditioning, and officiating the game of tennis are covered in this book. Review questions appear at the end of each chapter. Photographs. Drawings. Bibliography. Filmography.

302 Moore, William Edward. "Covert-overt service routines: the effect of a service routine training program on elite tennis players." Ed.D. Dissertation. Charlottesville, Virginia: University of Virginia, 1986. 114 p. UMI Order No. 8705719.

A covert-overt service routine training program was studied as a means of improving elite tennis players' service performance and routine adherence.

Morgenstern, Carol   see: Hines, Henry

Morris, Margaret   see: Lenglen, Suzanne

303 Morton, Jason; Seymour, Russell; and Burleson, Clyde. Winning tennis after forty. Englewood Cliffs, New Jersey: Prentice-Hall, 1980. 212 p. LC 79-19846. ISBN 0-13-961169-X.

The authors combine fifty years of playing and teaching experience to show senior players how to turn their skills and life experiences into winning tennis. Topics cover mental toughness, ball control, competition, exercising, and drills. Drawings.

Moss, Bill   see: Applewhaite, Charles

Mott, Mary L.   see: Mason, R. Elaine

304 Mottram, Anthony. Play better tennis. New York: Arco, 1971. 123 p. LC 70-161213. ISBN 0-668-02502-6.

Among featured aspects of this book are selecting the proper equipment, forehand and backhand grips, developing power and control with the forehand, the attacking backhand, receiving and returning the serve, how to play the lob and drop shot, correct positioning on the court, and effective practice methods. Photographs are arranged sequentially to provide a moving picture of strokes and footwork when the pages of the book are flipped foreward and backward quickly. Also published under the title Tackle tennis (London: Stanley Paul, 1975).

305 Mottram, Anthony. <u>Skills and tactics of tennis.</u> New York: Arco, 1980. 152 p. LC 79-18619. ISBN 0-668-04842-5.

The techniques involved in perfecting all the main strokes are fully explained in clear, easy-to-follow text which is illustrated with step-by-step photographs (color) and diagrams. This book also teaches the art of "courtcraft" and explains how to properly train and prepare for matches in a professional manner. Glossary.

Mullin, John   see: Fannin, Jim.

Murphy, Bill   see also: Murphy, Chet

306 Murphy, Bill. <u>Complete book of championship tennis drills.</u> West Nyack, New York: Parker, 1975. 228 p. LC 74-23175. ISBN 0-13-156000-X.

Individual and team drills are presented up to the level of championship play. Drills are grouped according to type of strokes and are listed in order of difficulty. An outline for teaching beginning tennis and checkpoints for basic strokes are included. Diagrams.

Murphy, Chester W.   see: Murphy, William E.

307 Murphy, Chet. <u>Advanced tennis.</u> 4th edition. Dubuque, Iowa: William C. Brown, 1988. 127 p. LC 88-70708. ISBN 0-679-07274-6.

This book is written for intermediate players and coaches looking for methods to improve performance. Emphasis is on flexible instruction. A new chapter covers "the geometry of impact," i.e., what happens when balls approach rackets at different angles and in different trajectories. Questions appear throughout the book to test readers' comprehension. Photographs. Diagrams. Index. Glossary. Sports and Fitness Series.

308 Murphy, Chet. Tennis for thinking players. 2nd edition. West Point, New York: Leisure, 1985. 176 p. LC 86-110387. ISBN 0-88011-251-4.

The author uses his years of experience teaching and coaching to help the reader discover those thoughts that will lead to mechanical soundness. Emphasis is on combining "brains and brawn."

309 Murphy, Chet, and Murphy, Bill. Tennis for the player, teacher and coach. Philadelphia: Saunders, 1975. 274 p. LC 74-17759. ISBN 0-7216-6620-5.

This is a "how-to-teach" tennis book. It describes how to teach the strokes, how to organize and conduct tennis classes, how to select varsity players for the team, how to teach tactics and strategy, and how to manage a scholastic or collegiate team. It combines theory with practical matters of teaching tennis. Contains an outline for teaching beginning tennis. Photographs. Diagrams. Bibliography. Glossary.

310 Murphy, William E., and Murphy, Chester W. Lifetime treasury of tested tennis tips: secrets of winning play. West Nyack, New York: Parker, 1978. 240 p. LC 77-17048. ISBN 0-13-536441-8.

Over two hundred instructional tips on stroke mechanics, tactics, strategy, the overhead, and other strokes are presented in this book. Diagrams.

311 Murray, H.A. Tennis for beginners. North Hollywood, California: Wilshire, 1976. 124 p. ISBN 0-87980-263-4.

The author discusses the pros and cons of different theories of teaching beginning strokes. The book is written so that beginners can easily follow the instruction. Diagrams. Index.

National Association for Sport and Physical Education see: Meinhardt, Tom

Navratilova, Martina   see also: Elstein, Rick

312 Navratilova, Martina, and Carillo, Mary. *Tennis my way*.
New York: Scribner's, 1983. 215 p. LC 83-11673. ISBN
0-684-18003-0.

Navratilova discusses tennis training and conditioning,
equipment, basic strokes, playing tactics and strategies, the mental aspects of the game, doubles, coaching, and other tennis topics. Photographs. Index.
Glossary.

Newcombe, Angie   see: Newcombe, John

313 Newcombe, John; Newcombe, Angie; and Mabry, Clarence.
The family tennis book. New York: Quadrangle, 1975.
157 p. LC 74-26011. ISBN 0-8129-0544-X.

This book presents the basics and explains how to use
these basics to develop a better game. A chapter
devoted to the family game covers practicing,
handicapping, conditioning, lessons, competition, and
setting goals. Photographs. Drawings.

Nieder, Lois Smith   see: Chavez, Rick.

Niemeyer, Jon Chalmers   see: Rhame, M. LeVan

314 Okker, Tom. *Tennis in pictures*. New York: Sterling,
1975. 160 p. LC 74-31696. ISBN 0-8069-4088-3.

Using clear stop-action sequential photographs, the
author leads the reader step-by-step through the basic
strokes. Each sequence shows the essential movement of
the strokes from the backswing, through contact with the
ball, to follow-through. Okker also covers tactics,
preparing for a match, how to recognize the crucial

point of a set, and how to plot percentage tennis.
Diagrams. Index. Glossary.

Old, Bruce S.   see: Talbert, William F.

Olderman, Murray   see: Van der Meer, Dennis

Oliver, Robert A.   see: Johnson, Dewayne J.

315   Orantes, Manolo, and Tarshis, Barry. <u>The steady game.</u>
New York: Bantam Books, 1977. 117 p. ISBN
0-553-11146-9.

This is a tactics book. The major idea expressed is
that the average player needs to base his game on
control and strategy. It is a guide to Orantes' style
of play - a style that emphasizes steadiness and variety
rather than power. Photographs.

316   Owens, Eleanor Boland. <u>Tennis: easy on - easy off.</u>
New York: United States Tennis Association, 1977. 70 p.

This publication illustrates a system for rapid placement of players on and off the court in round robin and
doubles-type play. Charts begin with 5 players on one
court and progress to a method of placing 32 players on
eight courts. For recreational leaders, tennis professionals, teachers, and coaches working with small or
large groups of individuals.

Ozier, Dan   see: Doerner, Cynthia.

317   Palfrey, Sarah. <u>Tennis for anyone!</u>   Revised edition.
New York: Cornerstone Library, 1980. 172 p. LC
81-102325. ISBN 0-346-12309-7.

The author combines instruction with past memories of former great women players. Levels of instruction vary from youth to adult players as the book progresses. Illustrated.

318   Paret, J. Parmly. _Lawn tennis as played by the champions._ New York: American Lawn Tennis, 1935. 80 p.

The special features of this book are the motion picture frames which accompany the instruction. Advanced playing techniques are provided by champions of the day and a course of lessons for beginners is written by the author.

319   Paret, J. Parmly. _Lawn tennis lessons for beginners._ 2nd edition. New York: American Lawn Tennis, 1926. 174 p. LC 26-12703.

A classic elementary book of instruction which teaches all the strokes of the game. Beginners' errors are carefully pointed out and detailed hints to guide beginners through the fundamentals of learning the game are presented. Photographs. The Lawn Tennis Library, Vol. I.

320   Paret, J. Parmly. _Mechanics of the game of lawn tennis._ New York: American Lawn Tennis, 1926. 269 p. LC 26-16237.

A classic guide to playing tennis after first principles have been mastered, this book contains a comprehensive analysis of all the motions used by expert players while making their shots. Photographs. The Lawn Tennis Library, Vol. II.

321   Paret, J. Parmly. _Psychology and advanced play of lawn tennis._ New York: American Lawn Tennis, 1927. 255 p. LC 27-11794.

A classic study of the secrets of the experts' skill in more advanced methods of tennis rather than the mere mechanical execution of shots. Includes diagrams and photographs of expert players in action. The Lawn Tennis Library, Vol. III.

322 Paret, J. Parmly, and Merrihew, S. Wallis. <u>Methods and players of modern lawn tennis</u>. 3rd edition. New York: American Lawn Tennis, 1931. 316 p. LC 31-9242.

Paret's classic book on tennis instruction covers all the fundamentals of the game. The unique feature of this book is the opinions from several expert players on disputed points of technique presented in the form of answers to questions posed by the authors. Photographs. The Lawn Tennis Library, Vol. IV.

323 Parks, Bradley A. <u>Tennis in a wheelchair</u>. Revised edition. Princeton, New Jersey: United States Tennis Association, 1988. 40 p.

The author, chairman of the National Foundation of Wheelchair Tennis, describes techniques for teaching and coaching wheelchair tennis. The basic strokes, racket work, wheelchair movement, and court position are covered. Photographs.

324 Paulson, Gary. <u>Forehanding and backhanding...if you're lucky</u>. Milwaukee: Raintree, 1978. 31 p. LC 77-27046. ISBN 0-8172-1158-6.

This book presents a commentary on several aspects of tennis with photographs (color) of famous players in unusual positions while playing tennis. Juvenile reading level.

325 Payne, Gloria. <u>Tennis for beginning and intermediate players</u>. 5th edition. Dubuque, Iowa: Kendall/Hunt, 1986. 51 p. LC 85-82534. ISBN 0-8403-3887-2.

Designed for use in college physical education classes, this book covers the language of tennis, basic and advanced strokes, the rules of tennis, and singles and doubles strategy. Photographs. Diagrams. Bibliography.

326 Payne, Martha S. "The construction of a volley test for aerial tennis." M.S. Thesis. Denton, Texas: North Texas State University, 1972. 54 p.

The purposes of this study were to construct a wall volley test for aerial tennis, to determine the reliability of the volley test, and to determine the validity of the volley test as an estimate of general playing ability of the individual performer in aerial tennis.

Pearce, Janice   see: Pearce, Wayne

327 Pearce, Wayne, and Pearce, Janice. Tennis. Englewood Cliffs, New Jersey: Prentice-Hall, 1971. 98 p. LC 79-149307. ISBN 0-13-903443-9.

While emphasizing the mechanical aspects of tennis, this book contains standard instruction on basic and advanced strokes. Also covers psychology, motor skills, and strategy. Diagrams. Drawings. Index. Bibliography. Glossary.

328 Pecore, Linda D. "A biomechanical analysis of the one-handed backhand groundstroke." M.S. Thesis. LaCrosse, Wisconsin: University of Wisconsin, 1978. 72 p.

The problem of this study was to biomechanically analyze the data of the performance of the one-handed backhand groundstroke for female beginning and advanced tennis players using the flexed (circular backswing) or the extended (straight backswing) elbow.

329 Peele, David A. Racket and paddle games, a guide to information sources. Detroit: Gale, 1980. 241 p. LC 80-23977. ISBN 0-8103-1480-0.

Although this bibliography covers a variety of racket sports, the majority of the 900 sources cited are on tennis. Each entry contains bibliographic information and a brief annotation. Subdivisions cover associations, audiovisual materials, books, periodicals,

Learning Tennis

instruction, rating systems, and tennis for the handicapped. Index.

330 Pelton, Barry C. Tennis. 4th edition. Glenview, Illinois: Scott, Foresman and Company, 1986. 126 p. LC 86-3692. ISBN 0-673-16665-1.

The author provides information on skill acquisition, techniques development, and tennis thinking, combined with his experience teaching and coaching tennis on the collegiate level. Photographs. Glossary.

331 Petro, Sharon. The tennis drill book. Champaign, Illinois: Leisure, 1986. 118 p. LC 84-47518. ISBN 0-88011-224-7.

The drills in this book are designed to help players make the transition from lessons to match play. Drills are grouped according to the primary stroke they are designed to develop. Within each group, the drills are arranged from the easiest to the most difficult. Photographs. Diagrams.

332 Petty, Roy. Contemporary tennis. Chicago: Contemporary Books, 1978. 104 p. LC 78-157. ISBN 0-8092-7458-1.

Primarily a book of fundamentals, the author presents his views about the use of wrist rotation on the topspin and backspin strokes. Discourages the two-handed backhand. Photographs. Diagrams. Glossary.

333 Phillips, Dorothy. Winning tennis. New York: Troll Associates, 1974. 32 p. LC 74-79100.

Very basic tennis instruction is illustrated in this book. Photographs (color) with brief descriptions cover the forehand, backhand, serve, and volley. Juvenile reading level.

334 Plagenhoef, Stanley. <u>Fundamentals of tennis</u>. Englewood Cliffs, New Jersey: Prentice-Hall, 1970. 130 p. LC 77-101530. ISBN 0-13-344606-9.

The mechanics associated with hitting a tennis ball are the focus of this book. Chapters cover grips; groundstrokes; the volley; the service and return of service; the smash and lob; and equipment design. An appendix includes technical treatments of ball flight, the striking mass of selected balls, the center of percussion, and racket data. Diagrams. Drawings. Index.

335 Platt, Don. <u>Tennis: playing a winning game</u>. Toronto: McGraw-Hill Ryerson, 1977. 103 p. LC C77-001082-2. ISBN 0-07-082511-4.

This book discusses the basics of grips and fundamental hitting techniques. Photographs are used heavily throughout the book to reinforce the author's points.

Pollard, Jack   see also: Laver, Rod

336 Pollard, Jack, editor. <u>Lawn tennis: the Australian way</u>. New York: Drake, 1973. 128 p. LC 72-6835. ISBN 0-87749-368-5.

Several former top Australian players have combined to set down in this book their attitudes, beliefs, and experiences on the court and in practice. Chapters deal with holding the racket, attacking on the forehand, how to practice, percentage tennis, singles strategy, left-handers, and tennis for middle-aged players. Photographs. Diagrams. Drawings.

337 Pons, Fred D. <u>Tennis made (somewhat) easier</u>. Jericho, New York: Exposition, 1973. 63 p. LC 73-90469. ISBN 0-682-47829-6.

The forehand backswing and follow-through, gripping the racket, proper footwork, accurate timing, volleying, serving, and the backhand are covered in a series of lessons. The author emphasizes the importance of off-court practice (stroking or swinging at imaginary balls at varying levels) as a means of improving stroke production. Photographs.

338 Poto, Carol Cosgrove. "Effect of ball velocity on spatial accuracy of the tennis volley." M.A. Thesis. Long Beach, California: California State University, 1984. 76 p.

This study examined the effect of ball velocity on spatial accuracy of the tennis volley to determine whether improvement in timing associated with stimulus velocity remains evident in a sport skill requiring both coincidental timing and aiming.

339 Powel, Col. Nick, editor. Friend at court. Revised edition. Lynn, Massachusetts: H.O. Zimman; dist. by the United States Tennis Association, 1989. 120 p.

This handbook is a guide for tennis officials. It includes duties of officials, solo chair umpire and mini-crew procedures, officiating techniques and tactics, USTA tournament regulations, the official Rules of tennis and cases and decisions (item no. 448), and The code (item no. 340). Diagrams. Index.

340 Powel, Col. Nick. The code. Revised. Lynn, Massachusetts: H.O. Zimman; dist. by the United States Tennis Association, 1989.

Contains the rules, principles, and guidelines which apply in any match conducted without officials. Index.

Poynder, Jane   see: Applewhaite, Charles

341 Professional Tennis Registry---USA. Instructor's manual, volume 2. Oakland, California: Professional Tennis Registry, 1978. 105 p.

Dennis Van der Meer demonstrates correct hitting methods in this book. Also includes advice on strategy and correcting faults. Photographs.

342 Pyles, James Edgar. "Tennis return of serve study with visual analysis." M.A. Thesis. Long Beach, California: California State University, 1977. 79 p. UMI Order No. 1311152.

The purpose of this study was to produce an instructional Super 8mm film entitled "Tennis Return of Serve Study with Visual Analysis." A review of literature disclosed that the return of serve is the most important aspect of tennis, yet the least understood and practiced.

343 Ralston, Dennis. Dennis Ralston's tennis workbook. Englewood Cliffs, New Jersey: Prentice-Hall, 1987. 187 p. LC 87-11524. ISBN 0-13-198607-4.

According to the author, this book will help the reader identify and correct specific game problems, reinforce previous knowledge in actual game play, and improve a player's game with each practice session. Emphasis is placed on balance, head movement, timing, tension level, and shot consistency. Photographs. Index. Checklists. Evaluation forms.

344 Ralston, Dennis, and Tarshis, Barry. Six weeks to a better level of tennis. New York: Simon and Schuster, 1977. 106 p. LC 77-3289. ISBN 0-671-22580-4.

The author emphasizes three keys to better tennis: early preparation; weight control; and proper racket work. A questionnaire to assist players in determining their playing level is included.

345 Ramo, Simon. Extraordinary tennis for the ordinary player. Revised edition. New York: Crown, 1977. 158 p. LC 76-30349. ISBN 0-517-55032-5.

This book is for the everyday player who wants to beat players of similar talent. The author uses humor to make some instructional points.

346 Ramo, Simon. Tennis by Machiavelli. New York: New American Library, 1984. 174 p. LC 85-7231. ISBN 0-452-25744-1.

A spoof translation of a sixteenth-century Niccolo Machiavelli manuscript. This book discusses the art of court psychology, strategies for ordinary play, and how to develop a winning attitude. Diagrams.

347 Ramsburg, I. Dale. "Anxiety, locus of control, and attributes to success/failure in a competitive tennis situation." Ed.D. Dissertation. Morgantown, Virginia: West Virginia University, 1978. 161 p. Order No. 7816991.

The major purposes of this study were: 1) to determine if individuals differed in their stated causal attributes to success or failure in a competitive tennis situation, and 2) to determine if these subjects' perceived causal attributes were related to their locus of control and trait anxiety.

Range, Peter Ross   see: Soules, George.

348 Ravielli, Anthony. What is tennis? New York: Atheneum, 1977. LC 77-1062. ISBN 0-689-30505-9.

This book covers groundstrokes and discusses the volley, lob, smash, and service. Includes a history of tennis. Drawings. Juvenile reading level.

349 Reardon, Maureen. Match point. Milwaukee: Advanced Learning Concepts, 1975. 75 p. LC 75-22012. ISBN 0-8172-0234-X.

This book is written for youngsters getting started in tennis. A player's first tournament experience is described. Also contains a brief history of the game and biographical material on tennis greats. Photographs. Juvenile reading level.

350 Reed, Rebecca Lee. "The influence of psychological stress and personality upon athletic performance of intercollegiate tennis players." M.S. Thesis. Denton, Texas: North Texas State University, 1978. 121 p. UMI Order No. 1311574.

This investigation was designed to study coach and self-appraised groupings of intercollegiate tennis players who yield to stress and withstand stress and to determine if personality differences existed between groups. A stress inventory and the Cattell Sixteen Personality Factor Questionnaire were instruments utilized in the study.

351 Reeves, Robert Milton. "The influence of a modified racket on the learning of certain fundamental tennis skills by young children." Ed.D. Dissertation. University, Alabama: University of Alabama, 1973. 129 p. UMI Order No. 749384.

The purpose of this study was to investigate the influence two different types of tennis rackets may have upon the learning of certain fundamental tennis skills by sixth grade boys and girls. The control group used a regular size racket and the experimental group used a training racket five inches shorter. The Broer-Miller Drive Test and the Hewitt Revision of the Dyer Backboard Test were used to measure performance.

352 Rhame, M. LeVan, and Niemeyer, Jon Chalmers. Tennis magic: playing with a full deck. New York: Vantage, 1979. 167 p. LC 78-055836. ISBN 0-533-03742-5.

The mental aspects of tennis are discussed in this book. Topics covered include tennis symbolism (choice of racket, shoes, etc.), how to analyze player personalities, and why some players move quickly from one instructor to another when taking lessons. Drawings. Bibliography.

353 Richmond, M. Barrie. Total tennis: the mind-body method. New York: Macmillan, 1980. 180 p. LC 79-24704. ISBN 0-02-603180-9.

The author's teaching philosophy of "total tennis" is presented in this book which combines the mental and physical aspects of the game. Of particular interest is the chapter on choking. Photographs. Index. Bibliography.

354 Riessen, Clare, and Cox, Mark. Tennis: a basic guide. New York: Lothrop, Lee, & Shepard, 1969. 128 p. LC 69-15859.

This guide explains the fundamentals and the finer points of tennis from a professional viewpoint. Pointers on grips, strokes, and techniques used by famous players are presented. Photographs. Index. Juvenile reading level.

355 Riley-Hagen, Margaret. "An analysis of the factors which distinguish tennis players of different serving abilities." M.S. Thesis. Denton, Texas: North Texas State University, 1985. 56 p. UMI Order No. 1326461.

The purpose of this study was to examine selected mechanical factors involved in the tennis serve. Special emphasis was placed on identifying factors which distinguish players of different serving abilities. Ten right-handed female tennis players, five ranked and five unranked, were evaluated, following filming with a high-speed camera, on the basis of five good and five fault serves.

356 Risman, Bev. Fit for tennis. London: B.T. Batsford Ltd., 1986. 94 p. LC 86-189701. ISBN 0-7134-4820-2.

The author believes skill in tennis is a product of fitness. This book is divided into three sections: general fitness; fitness for tennis; and ailments and injuries. Includes fitness tests and exercise routines. Photographs. Diagrams. Index.

357 Roberts, Betty Ruth. "The effect of two specific practice environments on the forehand and backhand ball placement ability of beginning tennis players." Ed.D. Dissertation. Greensboro, North Carolina: University of North Carolina, 1975. 101 p. UMI Order No. 7619419.

It was the purpose of this study to determine the effects of two practice environments on the forehand and backhand ball placement ability of beginning tennis players. Three tennis skills tests were administered during the study: the Shepard Modification of the Broer-Miller Tennis Drive Skills Test; the Hewitt Revision of the Dyer Backboard Test; and a Stationary Test.

358 Robertson, Max, and Kramer, Jack. The encyclopedia of tennis. New York: Viking, 1974. 392 p. LC 73-10776. ISBN 0-670-29408-X.

This volume provides the reader with a history of the game up to 1973, sections on instruction and great players, a collection of articles about tennis tournaments and organization, and a list of records of major championships. Photographs. Diagrams. Drawings.

Robinson, Louie, Jr. see: Ashe, Arthur.

359 Rosewall, Ken. Ken Rosewall on tennis. New York: Frederick Fell, 1978. 173 p. LC 78-18730. ISBN 0-8119-0309-5.

This book introduces beginners to the fundamentals of the game and offers advice gleaned from the author's own experiences. Photographs. Juvenile reading level.

360 Rosewall, Ken, and Barrett, John. Play tennis with Rosewall. North Hollywood, California: Wilshire, 1975. 160 p. LC 75-350013. ISBN 0-87980-305-3.

The author discusses choosing a racket, sensible tennis clothing, player movement on the court, footwork, balance, shot recovery, and proper stroking techniques. Also contains the author's memories of past matches and some of his famous opponents. Photographs. Diagrams.

361 Roswal, Glenn Morris. "A cinematographical analysis of one-handed and two-handed tennis backhand strokes." M.A. Thesis. Gainesville, Florida: University of Florida, 1974. 98 p.

The purpose of this study was to analyze the descriptive and mechanical variables of the conventional one-handed backhand stroke and the two-handed backhand stroke in tennis. Two descriptive and 24 quantitative variables were analyzed to provide a means of comparison.

Rotella, Robert J.   see also: Bunker, Linda K.

362 Rotella, Robert J., and Bunker, Linda K. "Research and future directions for the study of motor skill acquisition and performance in aging populations." 1979 13 p. ERIC Document No. ED 171704.

Two research designs are critically examined in this study. One study investigated field dependence and reaction time in senior tennis players. The other investigated concepts of locus of control and achievement motivation in highly successful male competitive tennis players age 65 and older. References are included.

363 Roy, Harcourt. Tennis for schools. London: Pelham Books, 1974. 226 p. LC 74-186347. ISBN 0-7207-0610-6.

This textbook is designed to help physical education specialists teach the fundamentals of tennis to children of all ages and abilities. Includes a description and explanation of padder-tennis, a game taught in British schools as a lead-in to tennis itself. Contains a sample lesson plan and various on-court group activities. Diagrams. Drawings. Index. Bibliography.

364 Sailes, Gary A. <u>Championship tennis drills for advanced players and coaches.</u> Chicago: Chicago State University, 1984. 104 p.

The author has compiled a collection of drills designed for the advanced player as well as the high school and college coach. The drills are organized as follows: baseline, net, serve and return of serve, doubles, and conditioning. Diagrams.

365 Sampedro, Renan Maximiliano Fernandes. "The anthropometric somatotype differences between male and female tennis players 10 to 14 years of age in the state of Tennessee." Ph.D. Dissertation. Nashville, Tennessee: George Peabody College for Teachers of Vanderbilt University, 1982. 168 p. UMI Order No. 8313849.

This study was designed to identify the major differences in the Health-Carter anthropometric somatotype of male and female ranked tennis players in the Tennessee Tennis Association between the ages of 10 to 14 years.

Sanders, Phronie   see: Shertenlieb, Bill.

366 Scholl, Peter. <u>How to succeed at tennis.</u> New York: Sterling, 1982. 127 p. LC 82-243242. ISBN 0-8069-4150-2.

Stroke techniques, the basics of singles and doubles tactics, how to train properly, and how to prepare for a match are discussed in this book. Photographs (color).

367 Schroer, Donald Paul. "Utilizing a 5 of 9 point tie-break as a determinant of playing ability for

Learning Tennis

college male tennis players." P.E.D. Dissertation. Bloomington, Indiana: Indiana University, 1974. 106 p. UMI Order No. 751546.

The problem of the study was to compare student rankings achieved through the use of a round robin tournament utilizing the USTA's approved 5 of 9 point tie-break to rankings achieved by subjective evaluation, results of a 7 of 12 point tie-break round robin tournament, and the Kemp-Vincent Rally Test.

368 Schultz, Nikki. Tennis for everyone. New York: Grosset and Dunlop, 1975. 96 p. LC 74-7544. ISBN 0-448-13231-1.

Standard instruction is presented in this book which covers practice techniques, basic strokes, specialty shots, etiquette, and strategy. Photographs. Glossary.

369 Schwed, Peter. How to talk tennis. New York: Dembner Books, 1988. 143 p. LC 87-30604. ISBN 0-942637-01-1.

This book provides the reader with a brief history of the game, profiles of top tennis stars, and definitions of terms from "ace" to "zip zip." Drawings. Index.

370 Schwed, Peter. The serve and the overhead smash. Garden City, New York: Doubleday, 1976. 86 p. LC 76-10521. ISBN 0-385-11487-7.

The author explains how to use different types of serves for maximum effectiveness and how to handle the overhead smash on different types of court surfaces. Diagrams. USTA Instructional Series.

371 Schwed, Peter. Sinister tennis: how to play against and with left-handers. Garden City, New York: Doubleday, 1975. 94 p. LC 73-20530. ISBN 0-385-06706-2.

The author provides the reader with advice on playing with and against left-handers in singles and doubles. Thinking opposite the usual playing pattern is advised when playing against such players. Diagrams. Drawings. USTA Instructional Series.

Scott, Eugene   see also: Duggan, Moira

372 Scott, Eugene. <u>Tennis: game of motion.</u> New York: Crown, 1973. 256 p. LC 72-82972. ISBN 0-517-50391-3.

Although this is not a how-to book, the vivid photographs (color) communicate the power and ferocity of the game. One chapter focuses on fundamental shots and includes photographs of some of the world's top players hitting forehand and backhand groundstrokes, the forehand and backhand volley, the serve, and the overhead.

373 Scott, Eugene, and DiGiacomo, Melchior. <u>The tennis experience.</u> New York: Larousse, 1979. 256 p. LC 79-7519. ISBN 0-88332-119-X.

This book attempts to convey in text and illustrations what the experience of playing tennis is like. Photographs of former tennis greats in their prime and in their early developmental stages are used to show the contrast in style and technique.

374 Scott, Eugene, and Lendl, Ivan. <u>Ivan Lendl's power tennis.</u> New York: Simon and Schuster, 1983. 120 p. LC 82-16962. ISBN 0-671-45908-2.

This book is filled with photographs of Lendl taken in competitive situations with his commentary about tuning up, groundstrokes, the service, net play, and the mental aspects of the game.

Sears, Ronald G.   see: Groppel, Jack L.

375 Sebolt, Don R. "The relationship of ball velocity and tennis playing ability of college men." P.E.D. Dissertation. Bloomington, Indiana: Indiana University, 1969. 128 p. UMI Order No. 702367.

The purpose of this study was to investigate the relationship between ball velocity and playing ability of beginning tennis players. The sampling unit used was comprised of 40 freshmen males randomly chosen from a pool of beginning tennis classes in the required physical education program at Virginia Polytechnic Institute, Blacksburg, Virginia. The Broer-Miller Tennis Achievement Test was used to measure performance.

376 Sebolt, Don R. Tennis. Revised edition. Dubuque, Iowa: Kendall/Hunt, 1974. 73 p. LC 75-131291. ISBN 0-8403-0266-5.

Standard instruction is presented in this book. One chapter describes a method of analyzing strokes based on cause and effect. Following each chapter is a list and definition of tennis terms. Photographs. Diagrams.

377 Secunda, Al. Ultimate tennis: the pleasure game. Englewood Cliffs, New Jersey: Prentice-Hall, 1984. 231 p. LC 84-015107. ISBN 0-13-935438-7.

This book is written for the beginner as well as the advanced player. Its most unique aspect deals with what a correct stroke should feel like rather than the exact physical reality of stroke production. Photographs.

378 Sedgman, Frank. How to play tennis. Wollstonecraft, Australia: Pollard, 1972. 128 p. LC 73-163303. ISBN 0-909950-12-1.

The author presents first a step-by-step outline of tennis basics followed by the subtle nuances of stroke production. Chapters cover grips and stances, developing a net game, court craft, and the doubles game. Photographs (color).

379 Sedgman, Frank. Winning tennis: the Australian way to a better tennis game. New York: Prentice-Hall, 1954. 132 p. LC 54-7754.

The author contends that mastering the fundamentals is the only way to enjoyable and winning tennis. Chapters cover grips, stances, basic strokes, net game, specialty shots, strategy, doubles, and equipment. Photographs.

380 Seewagen, George L., and Sullivan, George. Tennis. Chicago: Follett, 1968. 127 p. LC 67-10666.

The basics of the game of tennis are explained in this book. The principal strokes are emphasized - forehand, backhand, serve, and volley. Also covered are singles and doubles strategy and the Van Alen Simplified Scoring System (VASSS). Photographs. Diagrams. Juvenile reading level.

381 Segura, Pancho, and Heldman, Gladys. Pancho Segura's championship strategy: how to play winning tennis. New York: McGraw-Hill, 1976. 180 p. LC 75-43500. ISBN 0-07-056040-4.

The author covers all aspects of strategy. Chapters are divided according to the tennis ability of the reader. Drawings. Glossary.

382 Seixas, Vic, and Cohen, Joel. Prime time tennis: tennis for players over 40. New York: Scribner's, 1983. 239 p. LC 82-42660. ISBN 0-684-17904-0.

This book details everything of interest to the mature player including warmup techniques, court etiquette and psychology, effects of court surfaces and rackets on aging knees and elbows, and selecting a doubles partner. The author also takes the reader behind the scenes for glimpses of off-court personalities and tennis politics. Photographs. Index.

Seymour, Russell   see: Morton, Jason.

383 Shannon, Bill, editor. United States Tennis Association official encyclopedia of tennis. New York: Harper and Row, 1981. 558 p. LC 81-47237. ISBN 0-06-014896-9.

A tennis handbook containing chapters on the history of tennis, equipment, principles of tennis, rules and etiquette, results of major tournaments, and tennis greats. Photographs. Index. Glossary.

Shay, Arthur   see also: Groppel, Jack L.
                            Huang, Bob

384 Shay, Arthur. 40 common errors in tennis and how to correct them. Chicago: Contemporary Books, 1978. 100 p. LC 77-23708. ISBN 0-8092-7825-1.

Each error is illustrated, described in text, and diagnosed in this book. A correct photograph is shown for each mistake.

Sheehan, Larry   see also: Kramer, Jack
                            Smith, Stan

385 Sheehan, Larry, editor. Mastering your tennis strokes. New York: Atheneum, 1976. 201 p. LC 75-41854. ISBN 0-689-10718-8.

Hitting techniques for the serve, forehand, backhand, volley, and lob are described by former tennis stars. Correct and incorrect methods are illustrated to emphasize proper techniques. Photographs.

386 Shelton, Janice Carole. "Assertion in women's intercollegiate tennis." Ed.D. Dissertation. Greensboro, North Carolina: University of North Carolina, 1979. 144 p. UMI Order No. 8011213.

The broad purpose of this investigation was to study the assertive behaviors of women intercollegiate tennis players. The inquiry further sought to develop systematic observation techniques, a comparison between observed assertion in tennis play, team ranking, points and games won and lost, and compile player profiles which illustrate possible uses of observed findings.

387 Sherman, Patricia Ann. "A selected battery of tennis skill tests." Ph.D. Dissertation. Iowa City, Iowa: University of Iowa, 1972. 188 p. UMI Order No. 7226738.

The primary purpose of this study was to construct a battery of tennis skill tests with which to evaluate the achievements of beginning tennis students. The secondary purpose of the study was to construct a rating scale with which to measure tennis serving ability at the beginning level.

388 Shertenlieb, Bill, and Sanders, Phronie. Focus on competition: a tennis manual. Fort Lauderdale, Florida: Tennis Manual, 1978. 43 p.

This book is for anyone planning to organize tennis competition. The manual features challenge ladders, single/double elimination, playoff and consolation draws, tie-breakers, round robin tables from 3 to 24, social mixers, leagues, and simple handicapping. Illustrated.

Shields, Sharon L.   see: Johnson, Dewayne J.

389 Shingleton, Jack. How to increase your net value: a simplified guide to better tennis. New York: Winchester, 1975. 152 p. LC 74-16871. ISBN 0-87691-165-3.

The sections into which this book is divided cover each of the major strokes and grips, tips on the subtleties of tennis and how to avoid making errors, tournament play, doubles play, and tennis etiquette. Unique topics covered include how to play set point and how to adjust to adverse weather conditions. Photographs. Drawings. Index. Glossary. Cartoons.

Simon, Harvey B.   see: Levisohn, Steven R.

390 Singleton, Skip. <u>Intelligent tennis: a sensible approach to playing your best tennis...consistently.</u> White Hall, Virginia: Betterway, 1988. 158 p. LC 88-19346. ISBN 1-55870-102-8.

The aim of this book is to show how everyone can perform well on the tennis court by playing an intelligent game. The mental aspects of tennis are emphasized. Chapters cover self-control, concentration, self-image, effective practice methods, and the psychology of winning. For advanced players. Photographs. Index.

391 Sirota, Bud, and Gray, Howard C. <u>Direct tennis.</u> New York: Playmore, 1978. 96 p.

The authors present the concept of the racket as an extension of the arm and suggest that groundstrokes be taught with an open stance initially. Photographs. Drawings. Glossary.

Slatt, Bernie   see: Stein, Harold.

392 Smith, Charles. <u>An individualized instructional approach to tennis.</u> Dubuque, Iowa: Kendall/Hunt, 1981. 98 p. ISBN 0-8403-2365-4.

Designed for use at the high school or college level, this workbook contains behavioral objectives, materials for self-paced instruction, and learning activities for individualized instruction. Diagrams. Glossary. Tests. Crossword puzzle.

393 Smith, Gregory Lane. "A kinematic comparison of selected measures between two different part methods and the full tennis serve motion." M.S. Thesis. Fullerton, California: California State University, 1981. 50 p. UMI Order No. 1316454.

The purpose of this study was to analyze and compare selected aspects of two different part methods of the tennis serve, termed the short and modified serves, and to determine which part method was more similar to the full service motion.

394 Smith, Sarah Lynn. "Comparison of selected kinematic and kinetic parameters associated with the flat and slice serves of male intercollegiate tennis players." Ph.D. Dissertation. Bloomington, Indiana: Indiana University, 1979. 129 p. UMI Order No. 7921331.

The main purpose of this study was to describe and compare selected kinematic and kinetic parameters associated with the flat and slice serves. A secondary purpose was to study the relationship between total body COG and selected positions of the ball during the tossing component of the service.

395 Smith, Stan; Lutz, Bob, and Sheehan, Larry. Modern tennis doubles. New York: Atheneum/SMI, 1975. 150 p. LC 75-13514. ISBN 0-689-10687-4.

The principles of doubles play are presented. Topics include the importance of getting the first serve in, the chip backhand return, capturing the net, correct placement of volleys, and forming balanced doubles partnerships. Drawings.

396 Smith, Stan, and Sheehan, Larry. Stan Smith's guide to better tennis. New York: Grosset and Dunlop, 1975. 48 p. LC 75-621. ISBN 0-448-13278-8.

Common mistakes made by the weekend player are analyzed in this book. Smith provides remedies for serving without power, double-faulting, hitting groundstrokes into the net, lobbing too short, and poor footwork. Photographs (color). Drawings (color).

397 Smith, Stan, and Sheehan, Larry. Stan Smith's six tennis basics. New York: Atheneum, 1974. 48 p. LC 74-176280. ISBN 0-689-10636-X.

The basics discussed by Smith are to relax on the court, be ready, get the racket back quickly, keep eyes on the ball, hit the ball in front of the body, and follow-through completely. The two-handed backhand, doubles play strategy, and the psychological dimension of the game are also covered. Photographs (color).

398 Smith, Stan, and Valentine, Tom. Inside tennis. Chicago: Regnery, 1974. 91 p. LC 73-20692. ISBN 0-8092-8887-7.

This book covers the mechanics of the game from serving to volleying, strategy, winning tactics, and playing under various conditions. The Van Alen Simplified Scoring System (VASSS) is also explained. Photographs. Diagrams. Drawings. Index. Glossary.

Smyth Business Systems   see: United States Professional Tennis Association and Smyth Business Systems

399 Snyder, Dave. Tennis. Chicago: Athletic Institute, 1971. 48 p. LC 79-109498. ISBN 0-87670-049-0.

Basic tennis strokes are illustrated in this book. Includes a section on simplified rules and a self-evaluation test. Glossary.

400 Snyder, David William. "The relationship between the area of visual occlusion and groundstroke achievement of experienced tennis players." Ph.D. Dissertation. Columbus, Ohio: Ohio State University, 1969. 81 p. UMI Order No. 6922212.

This study experimentally analyzed experienced tennis players' groundstroking achievements under four different visual conditions and two ball speeds. An alternate form of the Broer-Miller Tennis Achievement

Test, which involved hitting 504 groundstrokes into target areas, was administered. Two Ball-Boy machines were used to throw tennis balls which the subject hit.

401 Soules, George, and Range, Peter Ross. <u>The playboy book of tennis: how to play winning tennis.</u> New York: Playboy, 1982. 237 p. LC 81-80401. ISBN 0-872237206.

The authors use a question and answer format to discuss the benefits of tennis, the importance of lessons, attending a tennis camp, selecting a partner, and fundamental strokes. Illustrated.

Special Olympics, Inc.   see: United States Tennis
   Association and Special Olympics, Inc.

402 Stein, Harold, and Slatt, Bernie. <u>Hitting blind: the new visual approach to winning tennis.</u> New York: Beaufort Books, 1981. 213 p. LC 81-04613. ISBN 0-8253-0061-4.

The visual responses to tennis are covered in depth in this book. The visual psychology of slow following eye movements and fast eye movements (saccades) are documented and applied to tennis. The authors answer the question, "Can you really keep your eye on the ball?" Photographs. Diagrams.

Stephens, Russell   see: Kleiman, Carol

402A Stern, Michele. "An integrated skills reinforcement program for beginning tennis." Ed.D. Dissertation. New York: Teachers College, Columbia University, 1988. 63 p. UMI Order No. 0563677.

This study is a presentation of a course in Beginning Tennis based upon the Integrated Skills Reinforcement model inclusive of assessment components. The tennis class is the context in which basic academic skills are introduced and integrated throughout the course content. This represents the first time a college physical activity course has been integrated with basic academic skills instruction.

Stolle, Fred   see also: King, Billie Jean

403 Stolle, Fred, and Appel, Martin. *Let's play tennis.* New York: Wanderer Books, 1980. LC 79-28061. ISBN 0-671330683.

This book discusses the rules, techniques, and necessary skills for the beginning tennis player. Index. Juvenile reading level.

404 Stranberg, Bo, and Jones, Ross. *Tennis the Swedish way.* Jonkoping, Sweden: NY-tryck Grafisha AB, 1983. 81 p.

The official coaching manual of the Swedish Tennis Association, this book breaks each stroke down to its grip, ready position, backswing, contact point, and follow-through. The techniques described and illustrated (color) produce a simple, uncomplicated line through the hitting area of each stroke to create a stroke pattern. Advice on tactics, conditioning, practice, and mental attitudes are also included.

Sullivan, George   see also: Seewagen, George L.

404A Sullivan, George. *Better tennis for boys and girls.* New York: Dodd, Mead, 1987. 62 p. LC 86-29123. ISBN 0-396-08939-9.

Discusses the rules, scoring, equipment, techniques, and tactics of tennis. Illustrated. Juvenile reading level.

405 Summerfield, Sidney C. *Tennis: learn to volley first.* New York: Vantage, 1970. 120 p.

The author reverses the usual order of tennis instruction by starting with the volley. Six different types of volleys are analyzed. Instruction also covers the overhead smash, serve, forehand drive, backhand drive, lob, half-volleys, and other speciality shots. Contains a chapter on teaching and coaching tennis. Drawings. Glossary.

406 Summers, Emery Floyd. "Tennis ability and its relationship to seven performance tasks." Ed.D. Dissertation. Eugene, Oregon: University of Oregon, 1973. 81 p. UMI Order No. 746904.

The primary purpose of this study was to establish the relationship between a battery of performance tasks and tennis playing ability. The tasks included: kinesthetic memory of varying hand positions; completion time of a short hand-arm movement; two choice reaction time; four choice reaction time; reciprocal tapping; a programmed movement; and a coincident timing task which involved meeting a moving target at a predetermined point with a hand-arm movement.

407 Sweeney, Karen. *Illustrated tennis dictionary for young people.* Englewood Cliffs, New Jersey: Prentice-Hall, 1979. 125 p. LC 78-73758. ISBN 0-13-451278-2.

The main part of this book is a dictionary which gives adequate definitions for most words. Also includes a section summarizing rules and the lives of some great players. Drawings. Juvenile reading level.

408 Swift, Betty Mae. "A skilled test and norms for the speed of the tennis serve." Ed.D. Dissertation. Fayetteville, Arkansas: University of Arkansas, 1969. 97 p. UMI Order No. 70398.

The purposes of this study were to devise a practical, reliable, and valid skill test for college women enrolled in beginning tennis to measure the speed of the ball on the serve (measured by time the ball was in the air) and to establish norms for this skill test.

409 Talbert, Bill. Sports Illustrated tennis. Revised edition. Philadelphia: J. B. Lippincott, 1972. 96 p. LC 72-37609. ISBN 0-397-00863-5.

The basics of tennis are summarized in three chapters which discuss singles, doubles, and mixed doubles. Instruction covers the grip, the volley, the forehand and backhand, and the importance of the serve. Techniques of effective net play, poaching, and the offensive and defensive lobs are also covered. Photographs. Diagrams. Drawings. Glossary.

410 Talbert, Peter, and Fishman, Lew. Secrets of a winning serve and return. Englewood Cliffs, New Jersey: Prentice-Hall, 1977. 191 p. LC 77-122. ISBN 0-13-797589-9.

Photographs of three different views of the serve are shown in this book: flat, slice, and twist. The author discusses how to anticipate the approaching serve and the proper return. Diagrams.

411 Talbert, William F., and Greer, Gordon. Bill Talbert's weekend tennis: how to have fun and win at the same time. Garden City, New York: Doubleday, 1970. 227 p. LC 77-103779. ISBN 0-385-08771-3.

Nontechnical advice for the average player is provided by the author. Areas covered include doubles, mixed doubles, the art of psyching, getting in shape, and family tennis. Drawings. Glossary.

412 Talbert, William F., and Old, Bruce S. The game of doubles in tennis. 4th edition. Philadelphia: J. B. Lippincott, 1977. 214 p. LC 77-35333. ISBN 0-397-00529-6.

This is a complete guide to doubles as all aspects of the game are covered. Diagrams.

413 Talbert, William F., and Old, Bruce S. The game of singles in tennis. Revised edition. Philadelphia: J. B. Lippincott, 1977. 158 p. LC 76-40118. ISBN 0-397-01181-4.

This is a book on the art of singles play. Statistics are included to show what percent of the time particular shots will win points. Diagrams.

414 Talbert, William F., and Old, Bruce S. Stroke production in the game of tennis. Philadelphia: J. B. Lippincott, 1971. 136 p. LC 77-151489. ISBN 0-397-00718-3.

The objective of this book is to provide a simple text on the fundamentals of tennis for coaches, teachers, and players. It concentrates on the methods of preparing for and executing the basic strokes. Diagrams. Drawings.

415 Talbert, William F., and Old, Bruce S. Tennis tactics: singles and doubles. New York: Harper and Row, 1983. 188 p. LC 82-48137. ISBN 0-06-015111-0.

Information on offensive and defensive play for singles and doubles is presented in this book. It covers serving basics on fast and slow courts, return-of-serve tactics, net play techniques, baseline forcing and passing shots, and an inspirational summary. Drawings.

416 Tantalo, Victor. USA tennis course. Orlando, Florida: USA Publishers, 1986. 202 p. LC 86-50302. ISBN 0-936577-01-0.

According to the author, this book provides the reader with a complete, structured course of study in tennis. It is comprised of 25 lessons designed to help players improve play without making any changes in stroke technique, select the proper style of play, and solve stroking problems. Drawings. Index.

Tarshis, Barry   see also: Laver, Rod
                              Orantes, Manolo
                              Ralston, Dennis

417 Tarshis, Barry. Tennis and the mind. New York: Atheneum, 1977. 183 p. LC 77-76789. ISBN 0-689-10749-8.

This book explores the mental facets of the game and is mostly composed of quoted material from interviews of famous players. Chapters cover controlling the mind, emotions on the court, tactics, and the winning edge. Bibliographic notes. A Tennis magazine book.

418 Tatje, Jerilyn Ann. "The effect of a short-handed tennis racket on the acquisition of basic tennis skills." M.S. Thesis. Urbana, Illinois: University of Illinois, 1970. 55 p.

The purpose of this study was to determine whether using a short-handed tennis racket facilitated the acquisition of basic tennis skills at the beginner's level by comparing the learning curves of groups using standard and short-handed rackets and by determining whether changing rackets produced positive or negative transfer.

419 Taylor, Charles David. "An electromyographic cinematographic analysis of the tennis serve." Ed.D. Dissertation. Blacksburg, Virginia: Virginia Polytechnic Institute and State University, 1978. 145 p. UMI Order No. 7822732.

This investigation was designed to observe systematically the extent of muscular involvement of selected arm and shoulder muscles of ten male varsity tennis players as they performed the twist, slice, and flat tennis serves.

420 "The teachers' guide to urban tennis instruction. The New York City schoolyard tennis program. Pilot program, Spring 1984." Brooklyn, New York: New York City Board

of Education, Division of Curriculum and Instruction, 1984. 46 p. ERIC Document No. ED 283906.

This guide is designed for New York City school teachers who conduct tennis classes for large groups of students while using limited tennis facilities. Plans for 24 half-hour lessons are presented with suggestions for equipment, aims, performance objecives, procedures, activities, and games. Prepared cooperatively with the New York Junior Tennis League and the USTA. Bibliography. Glossary.

421 Templeton, Gene Arden. "A comparison of an ideal tennis model and tennis performance." Ph.D. Dissertation. Albuquerque, New Mexico: University of New Mexico, 1970. 99 p. UMI Order No. 719323.

The objective of this investigation was to compare traditionally taught tennis skills and their elements with the skill elements reflected by three skill levels of tennis players in game situations. An Ideal Tennis Model of Skill Elements was devised through the use of expert opinion. Checklists for the forehand and backhand ground strokes and service were constructed from this model.

422 Tennis for women. New York: Doubleday, 1973. 245 p. LC 73-75416. ISBN 0-385-06727-5.

Several professional women players have combined to provide the reader with instruction in many aspects of the game. Topics covered include the forehand, backhand, serve, return of serve, overhead, volley, lob, drop shot, court strategy, women's doubles, and mixed doubles. Photographs.

423 Tennis Magazine. The tennis player's handbook. Norwalk, Connecticut: Golf Digest/Tennis; dist. by Simon and Schuster, 1980. 318 p. LC 79-65033. ISBN 0-914178-32-6.

This handbook contains information on how to choose equipment, clothing, camps, and a tennis instructor.

Learning Tennis   121

Advice on the avoidance and treatment of injuries and the advantages of private versus group lessons is also included. Photographs. Drawings.

424 Tennis strokes and strategies. New York: Simon and Schuster, 1975. 216 p. LC 75-14065. ISBN 0-671-22073-X.

The best of the "Instructional Portfolio" series of Tennis magazine is reproduced in this book. The material is divided into three categories: strokes, strategy, and practice/conditioning. Contributors include world-renowned players of the past. Photographs. Diagrams (color). Drawings.

425 Tilden, William Tatem. The art of lawn tennis. New York: George H. Doran, 1921. 175 p. LC 21-6269.

This book represents the author's theory of tennis techniques and his philosophy of court psychology. A chapter is devoted to the growth of modern tennis. Photographs.

426 Tilden, William Tatem. The expert: an analysis of tournament play. New York: American Sports, 1923. 62 p. LC 23-11047.

Tilden emphasizes the importance of psychology, tactics, and training in this volume. The author also discusses how to handle bad line calls, how to conserve energy during a match, and how to adjust style of play in competition. Photographs.

427 Tilden, William Tatem. Lawn tennis for club players. London: Methuen, 1922. 57 p. LC 41-2302.

The importance of practicing, footwork, and proper hitting techniques are emphasized in this book. Photographs.

428 Tilden, William Tatem. <u>Lawn tennis for young players</u>.
London: Methuen, 1922. 53 p.

This book contains a series of lessons for beginners covering sportsmanship, getting started in the game, holding the racket, and the basic hitting strokes. Photographs.

429 Tilden, William Tatem. <u>Match play and the spin of the ball</u>. Reprinted edition. New York: Arno, 1975. 177 p. LC 75-33763. ISBN 0-405-06679-1.

Tilden's classic book on the game of tennis contains a thorough discussion of the different types of spins and how to handle each. Also includes a biography of Tilden written by Stephen Wallis Merrihew and the author's opinion of various players of the 1920's. Photographs.

430 Tilmanis, Gundars. <u>Advanced tennis for coaches, teachers and players</u>. Philadelphia: Lea and Febiger, 1975. 126 p. LC 74-13856. ISBN 0-8121-0511-7.

This textbook is aimed at the adult learner. It provides coaches and teachers with detailed analysis of the mechanics involved in tennis. Topics include the biomechanical principles of tennis, class control and discipline, coaching methodology, activities for beginners, advanced physical fitness training, and singles, doubles, and mixed doubles tactics. Photographs. Diagrams. Glossary.

431 Trabert, Tony. <u>Tennis: how to play, how to win</u>.
Norwalk, Connecticut: Golf Digest/Tennis; dist. by Simon and Schuster, 1978. 222 p. LC 77-92906. ISBN 0-914178-19-9.

A series of articles from the "Instructional Portfolio" of <u>Tennis</u> magazine make up this book. Strokes are shown in sequential drawings. Each chapter blends photographs, drawings, and text to convey, simply and vividly, the mechanics of playing tennis successfully. Included are sections on strategy, practice, and conditioning.

432 Trabert, Tony, and Couzens, Gerald Secor. Trabert on tennis: the view from center court. Chicago: Contemporary Books, 1988. 209 p. LC 88-1835. ISBN 0-8092-4664-3.

Much of this book provides the reader with a behind-the-scenes look at modern tennis and its players. Trabert describes the physical and mental characteristics that make the difference between a winner and a loser. Diets, scientific training methods, the ideal tennis training program, effective practice routines, and court tactics are discussed. The Point System of the ATP and WITA is explained. Photographs.

433 Trabert, Tony, and Hook, Jim. The serve: key to winning tennis. New York: Dodd, Mead and Company, 1984. 140 p. LC 84-1510. ISBN 0-396-08298-X.

This book is devoted entirely to the serve. The authors stress the steps necessary to combine the component parts of the serve into a smooth, harmonious unit. Included are preparatory measures from the grip through the stance, preliminary motions from the respiration through the recovery, and propelling actions from the lift through the finish. Photographs. Diagrams.

434 Trabert, Tony, and Hyams, Joe. Winning tactics for weekend tennis. New York: Holt, Rinehart and Winston, 1972. 128 p. LC 77-185343. ISBN 0-03-091486-8.

Written in a question and answer format, this book delves into many aspects of the game of doubles. Topics discussed include the pre-game warm-up, the service, receiving the service, the volley, and basic strategy. Diagrams. Glossary.

435 Trane, Randy K. "A comparison of the personality traits of tennis coaches." M.S. Thesis. Provo, Utah: Brigham Young University, 1977. 54 p.

The problem of this study was to identify the personality characteristics of successful men's tennis coaches at the high school and college levels and to compare these to the personality characteristics of unsuccessful men's tennis coaches at the high school and college levels.

436 Trengove, Alan. <u>How to play tennis the professional way</u>. New York: Simon and Schuster, 1964. 160 p. LC 64-12480.

Ten former champions write about those particular features of tennis which have won them fame. The chapter by Rod Laver will be of particular interest to left-handed players. Photographs.

437 Truman, Christine. <u>Tennis</u>. Morristown, New Jersey: Silver Burdett, 1987. 64 p. LC 87-12946. ISBN 0-382-09489-1.

Coaching tips to help youngsters improve their tennis skills and tactics are offered in this book. Unique features include a brief diary of a female professional player, a description of major tennis stadiums, and the use of short tennis as a teaching method. Photographs (color). Index. Bibliography. Glossary. Juvenile reading level.

Tullius, John   see: Burwash, Peter

Tully, Shawn   see: MacCurdy, Doug

438 United States Professional Tennis Association. <u>How to hire a tennis professional</u>. Wesley Chapel, Florida: United States Professional Tennis Association, 1988. 34 p.

This book is written for readers in need of a tennis professional. It is designed to provide guidelines to help ensure that the best person available as well as the one who is right for the job is hired. Includes USPTA Code of Ethics and Tennis Professional Classifications, ten steps to follow to hire the best person, including a comprehensive series of forms, exhibits and guidelines to help find the right person to manage a tennis facility.

439 United States Professional Tennis Association. Tennis: a professional guide. New York: Kodansha International, 1984. 326 p. LC 84-846. ISBN 0-87011-682-7.

This book offers the knowledge and wisdom of 24 outstanding tennis teaching professionals. It was published to help the USPTA achieve its two-fold purpose to create and stimulate a greater awareness in the game of tennis and to upgrade the standards of the teaching profession. Photographs (color). Diagrams. Index. Glossary. The Official Handbook of the United States Professional Tennis Association.

440 United States Professional Tennis Association. The USPTA complete guide to coaching, volume 1. Wesley Chapel, Florida: United States Professional Tennis Association, 1987. 135 p.

The requirements for becoming a tennis professional from a coaching perspective are outlined in this book. Chapters cover the new coach; coaching philosophy; recruiting; coping with peer pressure; communicating with the coach and defining goals in a college environment; coaching sportsmanship; and self improvement for the coach. Photographs. Charts.

441 United States Professional Tennis Association. The USPTA junior development manual, volume 1. Wesley Chapel, Florida: United States Professional Tennis Association, 1986. 80 p.

This book contains the teaching and writing expertise of several USPTA members. Teaching professionals looking for practical advice on developing a junior tennis program will find this book useful. Chapters cover program development; marketing and promotion; teaching the proper attitude, discipline and sportsmanship; biomechanical and sports medicine for junior players; developing the tournament player; and setting up a successful training program. A tennis resources chapter provides information on different types of resources available to coaches and teachers. Photographs. Charts.

442 United States Professional Tennis Association. The USPTA sport science and sports medicine guide, volume 1. Wesley Chapel, Florida: United States Professional Tennis Association, 1988. 162 p.

This handbook details the sport science and sports medicine implications of playing tennis and individualizing a training program for the competitive tennis player. Chapters cover biomechanical aspects of player development, orthopedic concerns for the tennis professional, rehabilitative concerns following injury or surgery, weight training, conditioning, nutrition, ergogenic aids, preventing and treating injuries of the foot, psychological aspects of teaching and coaching tennis, sex differences and skill acquisition, and competitive stress on the junior level. Contributions were made by some of the world's top authorities in the field. Photographs. Drawings. References and Recommended Readings.

443 United States Professional Tennis Association. The USPTA tennis professional's business manual. Wesley Chapel, Florida: United States Professional Tennis Association, 1985. 112 p.

The essentials of the business of the tennis teaching profession are described in this book. Topics covered include writing a tennis resume, successful interviewing, negotiating a contract, implementing an accounting program for a pro shop, public relations, estate planning for the tennis professional, and how to get published. Photographs.

444 United States Professional Tennis Association and Smyth Business Systems. The USPTA accounting, business and financial management handbook. Wesley Chapel, Florida: United States Professional Tennis Association, 1987.

This handbook explains basic accounting concepts, procedures for controlling accounts payable, procedures for paying employees, how to record sales and related sales transactions, methods of controlling and managing inventory, methods of issuing and controlling credit, how to finance a tennis shop, basic tax and legal considerations, and how to evaluate the financial performance of a tennis shop.

445 United States Tennis Association. COURTSTAR program. New York: United States Tennis Association, 1980.

Designed especially for group teaching in schools, parks, and community centers, this kit contains a pre-planned lesson agenda for teaching beginners. Includes leadership tests, class roll forms, and test cards for students.

446 United States Tennis Association. A handbook for chairmen of junior tennis tournaments. New York: United States Tennis Association, 1984. 55 p.

This publication is a guide to the planning of junior tournaments. Especially directed to the novice chairman.

447 United States Tennis Association. A handbook for junior tennis tournament players. Revised edition. New York: United States Tennis Association, 1984. 52 p. ISBN 0-938822-68-3.

Tournament procedures, rules of match play, and etiquette for the new competitor are covered in this publication. Drawings.

448 United States Tennis Association. Rules of tennis and cases and decisions. Lynn, Massachusetts: H. O. Zimman: dist. by the United States Tennis Association, 1989. 28 p.

This pamphlet contains the official rules of the International Tennis Federation of which the USTA is a member. Included are "Comments" by the USTA Tennis Rules Committee which amplify and facilitate interpretation of the formal code. Index.

449   United States Tennis Association. Starter tennis. New York: United States Tennis Association, 1985. Revised.

This is an elementary instructional program developed by the USTA for use by groups with limited tennis facilities. The package includes a teacher's guide, booklets, skill tests, certificates, and badges for students.

450   United States Tennis Association. Tennis programs for the disabled. Revised edition. New York: United States Tennis Association, 1986. 70 p.

This is a guide for organizations and individuals interested in offering tennis activities for the disabled. It includes how-to sections on teaching tennis to disabled athletes, guidelines on starting programs, and a state-by-state directory of current programs.

451   United States Tennis Association. USTA college tennis guide, 1988-89. 6th edition. New York: United States Tennis Association, 1988. 45 p.

For the college-bound tennis player, this book contains a comprehensive list of universities, colleges, and junior colleges that offer tennis programs and scholarships. Also contained are brief descriptions of national collegiate athletic associations and the results of national championships. Additional publications list.

452   United States Tennis Association. The USTA guide to forming a community tennis association. New York: United States Tennis Association, 1985. 54 p.

Information on how to organize recreational tennis programs for players of all ages and abilities is contained in this book. Detailed information on how to formalize the administrative structure and incorporate as a non profit organization with tax-exempt status is also provided. Illustrated.

453 United States Tennis Association. **USTA guide to fund raising for community tennis associations.** New York: United States Tennis Association, 1985. 56 p.

The basic steps and strategies necessary to implement and maintain an effective fund raising program are outlined in this book. Contains practical ideas for planning and running fund raising events. Illustrated.

454 United States Tennis Association. **USTA schools program tennis curriculum.** 2nd edition. New York: United States Tennis Association, 1986. 73 p.

A guide to teaching tennis in the schools, this publication includes practical tips on games and activities for large groups with limited facilities. Photographs. Bibliography. Evaluation forms. Skill tests.

455 United States Tennis Association. **USTA score book for coaches.** New York: United States Tennis Association, 1984.

This publication is designed for high school and college coaches, officials associated with camps, clubs, and community tennis programs, and others utilizing a team format for competition. As a complete record book, it contains charts for match schedules and individual records, team rosters, round robin forms, and more.

456 United States Tennis Association. **USTA senior tennis directory.** New York: United States Tennis Association, 1988.

This is a resource guide for organizations interested in offering tennis programs for seniors. The guide contains articles by renowned specialists on why seniors play tennis, guidelines for developing successful programs, and a research-based directory of 250 local activities for seniors.

457 United States Tennis Association. USTA short tennis: leader's guide to short tennis intramurals. New York: United States Tennis Association, 1988. 17 p.

Guidelines for the development and implementation of a short tennis program as an option for intramural sports in grade schools and junior highs are contained in this pamphlet. Sections cover how to get the program underway, court dimensions and equipment specifications, how to play short tennis, group games and activities, and resources available from the USTA. Photographs. Diagrams.

458 United States Tennis Association. USTA SPORTSTAR kit. New York: United States Tennis Association, 1984.

This package contains a complete program for developing a positive attitude toward tennis rules, conduct, and competition. Recommended for players in grade school through high school.

459 United States Tennis Association. USTA tennis camp/clinic directory. New York: United States Tennis Association, 1988.

A directory of more than 300 camps and academies around the world for adults and junior players. Each entry includes the location, address, telephone number, number of courts, student/instructor ratio, level of instruction, length and dates of sessions, and cost.

460 United States Tennis Association. USTA tennis films. New York: United States Tennis Association, 1987. 40 p. ISBN 0-938822-71-3.

The USTA Tennis Film List and National Film Library are combined in one volume in this work which indexes over

140 films and videotapes. Titles are categorized as instructional, match highlights, and tennis miscellany. Includes addresses of USTA Sections and District Film Libraries.

461 United States Tennis Association. USTA tennis in the parks curriculum. New York: United States Tennis Association, 1987. 67 p.

This guide is designed for parks and recreation department tennis program administrators and teachers. It is comprised of a series of 30 group lesson agendas, each of which gives the teacher a minute-by-minute schedule and guidelines for conducting games and drills. A companion volume to the USTA schools program tennis curriculum (item no. 454). Diagrams.

462 United States Tennis Association. USTA tennis publications. New York: United States Tennis Association, 1988. 24 p.

This catalog contains a selective list of outstanding tennis publications. Materials are classified by subject and a brief description follows each title. The catalog's objective is to identify quality educational materials which will contribute to the development of the finest teaching programs, recreational activities, facilities, and tournaments for every player. Illustrated. Order form included.

463 United States Tennis Association. Welcome volunteers. New York: United States Tennis Association, 1987. 16 p.

The USTA's organizational structure is briefly outlined in this pamphlet. The many ways in which volunteers can participate in tennis activities is discussed. Illustrated.

464 United States Tennis Association and Special Olympics, Inc. Special Olympics tennis sports skills guide. New York: United States Tennis Association, 1987. 64 p.

Coaching criteria and guidelines for Special Olympics tennis coaches are outlined in this publication. It contains tips for conditioning drills, basic racket skills, stroking techniques, and match-play concepts. Designed for all levels of coaching. Diagrams. Drawings. Bibliography. Glossary.

Valentine, Tom   see: Smith, Stan

465   Van der Meer, Dennis. Dennis Van der Meer's complete book of tennis. Ottawa, Illinois: Green Hill; dist. by Kampmann and Company, 1986. 300 p. LC 82-80144. ISBN 0-915463-33-4.

This book illustrates the author's method of scientifically teaching tennis in progressive steps from simple to complex. It is based on biomechanical principles and sound techniques. All the basics and speciality shots are covered, in addition to chapters on tactics, drills, physical conditioning, the mental side of tennis, and how to teach children. Photographs.

466   Van der Meer, Dennis, and Olderman, Murray. Tennis clinic: play the TennisAmerica way. New York: Hawthorn, 1974. 193 p. LC 74-347. ISBN 0-8015-7524-9.

The teaching methods of Van der Meer are presented in this clinic simulation which takes the reader from learning the basic strokes, to understanding tennis psychology, to developing a winning style. Photographs. Index.

467   Van Kanegan, Steve. Optic yellow fever: treat tennis as a game and you'll get better. Los Alamitos, California: S.V. Wingit, 1984. 153 p.

In prose style, the author combines his love for and experience playing tennis with tips and advice on getting started, practicing, club and tournament competition, and stroking mechanics. This is an unconventional instruction book which combines cartoons with a casual approach to learning the game.

468 Van Noord, Nancy Lynn. "Development and evaluation of a self-talk assessment instrument for tennis players." Ph.D. Dissertation. East Lansing, Michigan: Michigan State University, 1984. 211 p. UMI Order No. 8507554.

The purpose of this investigation was to design a self-talk questionnaire (STQ) which could validly and reliably assess the type and frequency of a tennis player's competition-related self-talk as it related to competitive psychological effectiveness. A valid and reliable 51-item self-talk questionnaire (STQ-3) was developed which evolved from the sequential construction and later administration of the STQ-1 and STQ-2.

469 Van Schoyck, Stephen Roger. "Cognitive processes in tennis players: test of three factors." Ph.D. Dissertation. Cincinnati, Ohio: University of Cincinnati, 1984. 211 p. UMI Order No. 8413711.

This study emphasized the self-report of athletes to define the cognitive dimensions that mediate sport performance. Three factors (scan, focus, and absorption) were identified and examined relative to tennis skill.

470 Varn, Ben. Stairsteps to successful tennis. Second edition. Travelers Rest, South Carolina: Tennis Services Company, 1983. 274 p. LC 74-27861. ISBN 0-9601310-1-9.

The SST Progression Plan is presented in this book. The Plan consists of nine stairsteps each utilizing the building block approach to teaching. It specifies the strokes and strategy a player must learn to consistently execute properly the various strokes. Each stairstep contains objectives, instruction, and strategies for implementation. Also contains a chapter on the principles for successful doubles. Photographs. Diagrams. Glossary.

Vasil, Elizabeth   see: Fox, John

471 Veilleux, Dave. "Physical education: tennis, physical fitness, body-building." 1979. 9 p. ERIC Document No. ED 175836.

This unit plan for introducing high school students to the game of tennis is divided into objectives and suggested activities. Student evaluation procedures are outlined and a sample evaluation checklist is provided.

472 Vicory, James Ray. "Delayed augmented feedback: the usefulness as perceived by intercollegiate tennis athletes." Ed.D. Dissertation. Provo, Utah: Brigham Young University, 1979. 170 p. UMI Order No. 8000094.

The purpose of this tudy was to determine the usefulness, as perceived by highly skilled college athletes, of delayed augmented feedback presented by a microcomputer and tennis analysis system.

Vier, Gene   see: Vines, Ellsworth

473 Vines, Ellsworth. Ellsworth Vines' quick way to better tennis: a practical book on tennis for men and women. New York: Sun Dial, 1939.

Photographs and descriptive text dominate this folio volume in which the author's hitting techniques are illustrated and described. Emphasis is placed on proper grips, the manner in which the eyes follow the ball, balance, and footwork.

474 Vines, Ellsworth. How to play better tennis. Philadelphia: David McKay, 1938. 119 p. LC 38-19736.

Basic strokes executed by the author are illustrated in this book. Emphasis is placed on watching the ball and using the proper grips. Photographs.

475 Vines, Ellsworth. Tennis simplified for everyone. New York: American Sports, 1933. 125 p. LC 33-21765.

In an effort to present tennis fundamentals and facts in their simplest form, the author uses the question and answer method. Chapters cover the forehand and backhand drives, service, lob, volley, gripping the racket, and developing accuracy. Photographs. Diagrams. Glossary. Juvenile reading level.

476 Vines, Ellsworth, and Vier, Gene. Tennis: myth and method. New York: Viking, 1978. 320 p. LC 77-18544. ISBN 0-670-69665-X.

The authors rank and discuss the ten greatest players in tennis. Instructional tips for intermediate and advanced players are included. Photographs. Drawings. Glossary.

477 Wagenvoord, James. Tennis notes. New York: St. Martin, 1981. 160 p. LC 81-377. ISBN 0-312-79104-6.

This book consists of brief, informative sections designed to increase the reader's knowledge of tennis. Most of the book contains log sheets to be used to record notes about matches, lessons, equipment, and names and addresses. Reading list. Drawings.

Walts, Kenneth   see: Mason, R. Elaine

478 Watauabe, Dennis. "Explanation paradigms: their application potential in the field of tennis instruction." Ph.D. Dissertation. Chicago: Loyola University of Chicago, 1977. 127 p. UMI Order No. 7713438.

This study presents a comprehensive explanation paradigm for tennis instruction. It is based on a three stage instructional sequence. The first two stages involve a learner who is still struggling to acquire the basic skills. The third stage has applicability to the same learner at a more advanced stage in his learning experience.

479 Weinberg, Robert S. The mental advantage: developing your psychological skills in tennis. Champaign, Illinois: Leisure, 1987. 209 p. LC 87-3722. ISBN 0-88011-293-X.

The objectives of this book are to educate players and coaches about the importance of psychological training, to describe the psychological states associated with peak performance, to discuss the development of psychological skills, and to detail specific techniques, strategies, and programs to practice developing psychological skills. Photographs. Drawings. Index.

480 Wells, Ward Tom. "The effect of the graduated length method on tennis achievement of beginners." P.E.D. Dissertation. Bloomington, Indiana: Indiana University, 1981. 109 p. UMI Order No. 8221544.

The purpose of this study was to determine the effectiveness of learning beginning tennis skills through the use of the Graduated Length Method. This method of instruction used four progressions that varied implement length used by the learner.

Weymuller, Frederick   see: Faulkner, Edwin J.

481 Whittaker, Sharon Anne. "Nonverbal communication of winning and losing in tennis." Ph.D. Dissertation. Seattle, Washington: University of Washington, 1980. 331 p. UMI Order No. 8109786.

The purpose of this research was to compare ability of experienced and inexperienced tennis players (decoders) in assessing the relevant nonverbal information within behavioral sequences of selected encoders and to identify the essential components of both the winning and losing behavioral display.

482 Wightman, Hazel Hotchkiss. Better tennis. New York: Houghton Mifflin, 1933. 131 p. LC 33-13972.

The author outlines the techniques and strategies for women players to follow to develop a competitive game. Contains a list of tennis slogans and maxims. Also includes biographical sketches of some of Wightman's contemporaries. Photographs. Glossary.

Williams, Joanne   see: Blaskower, Pat

Williams, Roger   see: Bunis, Alvin W.

483 Willis, De Witt. Learn to play tennis at home. New York: McGraw-Hill, 1976. 118 p. LC 76-5941. ISBN 0-07-070625-5.

The author presents aspiring players a system for muscle training and practicing strokes off the court. Illustrations compose the bulk of the book.

484 Wills, Helen. Tennis. New York: Scribner's, 1928. 214 p. LC 28-12201.

Wills discusses the value of tennis and setting goals before describing her techniques on the strokes, net game, tactics and strategy, and the ideal temperament for competitive tennis. Drawings.

485 Wilson, Craig R. How to improve your tennis: style, strategy, and analysis. Cranbury, New Jersey: A.S. Barnes, 1974. 205 p. LC 73-17465. ISBN 0-498-01483-5.

This book progresses systematically from the practical aspects of stroke development, through a detailed study of percentage decision-making on the court, to the strategy and tactics necessary to compete successfully in tournament-level competition. It concludes with a theoretical model to objectify both individual career development and competition performance. Photographs. Diagrams.

486 Wilson, Craig R. Tennis: beyond the inner game. New York: Drake, 1977. 143 p. LC 76-27798. ISBN 0-8473-1361-1.

This book explores the notion that self-mastery is a lifelong pursuit which can take place in any medium which taxes the human spirit, including the game of tennis. It analyzes the meditative approach to life and the spirit of tennis. Includes biographical material of top ranked players. Photographs.

487 Wilson, Craig R. Total health tennis: a lifestyle approach. Ardmore, Pennsylvania: Whitmore, 1979. 159 p. LC 79-51336. ISBN 0-87426-050-7.

The notion of sport as a metaphor for life is the concept advocated in this book. The author believes tennis can serve as the basis for sound physical and mental health. According to Wilson, using the philosophy, techniques, and exercises presented, the reader can become not only a better player but a successful person in life itself.

488 Winnett, Tom, and Fay, Marion. Tennis is an unnatural act. Berkeley, California: Wilderness, 1977. 99 p. LC 77-71716. ISBN 0-911824-60-X.

The authors believe movements required in tennis are unnatural and must be learned. The importance of inner calmness is also discussed.

489 Wood, Daniel T. Tennis for the university student from recreation to competition. Dubuque, Iowa: Eddie Bowers, 1982. 122 p. ISBN 0-912855-35-5.

This book is designed to give players options and choices that may help them to enjoy the many physical, social, and mental rewards of tennis. The chapters are designed to improve skills quickly, prevent injuries, and provide a lifelong sport. Photographs. Diagrams. Bibliography. Glossary.

490 Woods, Ronald B. "The effect of music on the learning of tennis skills." Ph.D. Dissertation. Philadelphia: Temple University, 1976. 75 p. UMI Order No. 7622131.

The purpose of this study was to investigate the effect of popular music on the learning of selected tennis skills. A sub-problem was to determine the effect of the music upon the attitude of the subjects toward learning tennis skills.

491 Woods, Ronald B. *Your advantage: a textbook for students and teachers of tennis.* Dubuque, Iowa: Kendall/Hunt, 1976. 78 p. ISBN 0-8403-1325-X.

This text is the result of the author's experience teaching and coaching tennis. It provides the reader with a complete introductory course in tennis. Instruction is presented in concise outline form. Included is a chapter on teaching progressions. Diagrams. Bibliography. Glossary. Test. Student Questionnaire.

492 Wright, Bill. *Aerobic tennis.* Bolinas, California: Shelter Publications, 1983. 189 p. LC 83-510. ISBN 0-936070-02-1.

This book illustrates and describes how tennis can give the reader a superb aerobic workout, improve overall fitness, strength, and agility. It presents a new look at an old game.

Xanthos, Paul J.   see also: Johnson, Joan D.

493 Xanthos, Paul J. *Organization and conduct of tennis clinics and teacher training workshops.* New York: United States Tennis Association, 1981. 39 p. LC 87-401530. ISBN 0-938822-03-9.

This pamphlet is written for those planning tennis clinics and workshops. It includes preliminary program planning, budgeting, staffing, and sample formats for one-day, three-day, and five-day workshops for teachers. Photographs. Bibliography.

494 Yale, Virginia, and Lewis, Morey. Solo tennis. New York: Drake, 1976. 94 p. LC 75-36142. ISBN 0-8473-1062-0.

The benefits of practicing against a backboard are advocated in this book. Photographs. Diagrams.

495 Yeo, David G. "Tennis: course proposal." Philadelphia: Philadelphia Community College, 1985. 87 p. ERIC Document No. ED 267831.

This course was designed to provide instruction and practice in the basic tennis techniques of the forehand, backhand, serve, volley, and overhead. Includes course goals, objectives, and outline. Glossary. Exams. Assignments.

496 Young, Charles R. Winning weekend tennis. Detroit: Harlo, 1981. 112 p. ISBN 0-8187-0044-0.

The author, a tennis enthusiast, offers advice and opinions based on his personal experiences and knowledge of the game. The book covers both singles and doubles play. Drawings.

497 Young, Gloria M. "An analysis of selected mechanical factors and accuracy in tennis strokes as related to ball velocity and skill level." Ed.D. Dissertation. Philadelphia: Temple University, 1970. 132 p. UMI Order No. 7110841.

The purpose of this study was 1) to determine the effect of ball velocity on the accuracy of the tennis forehand and backhand of novice and advanced players, and 2) to determine the effect of ball velocity on selected mechanical factors of the tennis forehand and backhand of novice and advanced players. Factors analyzed were ball velocity, knee flexion, racket angle, subject distance from the ball, racket movement, shoulder angle, pelvic rotation, and spinal rotation.

498 Young, Gloria M. Mechanics of tennis. Riverside, California: Tennis Ink, 1978. 85 p.

The author presents an analysis of each stroke in terms of the mechanics of movement involved. Photographs. Index. Bibliography.

499 Youth Tennis Foundation of Southern California. Ten tests for better tennis. Los Angeles: Kellow-Brown, 1979. 24 p.

This pamphlet contains handy tips and exercises to help students learn to become better tennis players. Useful to instructors and parents in schools, camps, and scout groups. Illustrated.

500 Zebas, Carole J., and Johnson, H. Mardi. Tennis: back to the basics. Dubuque, Iowa: Eddie Bowers, 1987. 117 p. ISBN 0-912855-72-X.

The objective of this book is to provide information for players and teachers on the fundamentals of stroke development and analysis. One chapter is devoted to keying in on the movement patterns most likely to be altered during an unsuccessful tennis stroke. Also includes sections on practice drills, strategy, and conditioning. Photographs. Diagrams. Glossary. Checklists.

501 Zwieg, John, and Isaacs, Richard S. Courtside companion: a tennis workbook for the serious player. San Francisco: Chronicle Books, 1973. 91 p. LC 73-77334. ISBN 0-87701-042-0.

Filled with sequence photographs of each stroke, this book provides a step-by-step review of the essential elements involved in properly executing the strokes in tennis. Tips on how to practice, how to win, conditioning, and using drills to improve are also included. Photographs. Index. Glossary.

TITLE INDEX

The number following each title refers to the entry number in the bibliography.

Achievement in tennis skills as related to different scheduling patterns (M.S.) **298**

Advanced tennis (Metzler) **292**

Advanced tennis (Murphy) **307**

Advanced tennis for coaches, teachers, and players **430**

Advantage tennis: racket work, tactics, and logic **18**

Aerobic tennis **492**

America's tennis book **66**

Anaerobic and aerobic capacity of selected Southern California female collegiate skilled and unskilled tennis players (M.S.) **284**

An analysis of selected mechanical factors and accuracy in tennis strokes as related to ball velocity and skill level (Ed.D.) **497**

An analysis of service effectiveness in championship men's tennis (Ed.D.) **180**

An analysis of the factors which distinguish tennis players of different serving abilities (M.S.) **355**

An analysis of the visual/perceptual attributes of male and female tennis players of varying ability levels (Ed.D.) **29**

The anatomy and psychology of tennis **117**

The anthropometric somatotype differences between male and female tennis players 10 to 14 years of age in the state of Tennessee (Ph.D.) **365**

An anthropometric, somatotypological and physiological study of tennis players with special reference to the effects of training (Ph.D.)   **81**

Anxiety, locus of control, and attributes to success/failure in a competitive tennis situation (Ed.D.)   **347**

The art and science of tennis   **111**

The art of lawn tennis   **425**

Arthur Ashe's tennis clinic   **11**

Assertion in women's intercollegiate tennis (Ed.D.)   **386**

Assessing perception of object directionality in tennis (Ph.D.)   **112**

Ball persons: a trainer's manual   **188**

The basic strokes   **93**

Basic tennis illustrated   **87**

Bathroom tennis: 8 minutes a day to learn, improve and maintain your tennis game at home   **35**

Be a winner in tennis   **80**

Beginners guide to winning tennis   **192**

A behavioral analysis of more and less successful high school tennis coaches (Ed.D.)   **72**

Better tennis (Crooke)   **85**

Better tennis (Wightman)   **482**

Better tennis for boys and girls (Hopman)   **182**

Better tennis for boys and girls (Sullivan)   **404A**

Bill Talbert's weekend tennis: how to have fun and win at the same time   **411**

Billie Jean King's secrets of winning tennis   **215**

A biomechanical analysis of the one-handed backhand groundstroke (M.S.)   **328**

The book of tennis: how to play the game   **270**

Boris Becker's tennis: the making of a champion   **46**

Bud Collins' modern encyclopedia of tennis   **74**

Budge on tennis   **55**

Championship tennis drills for advanced players and coaches **364**

Championship tennis by the experts, how to play championship tennis **13**

Checklist for better tennis **31**

A cinematographical analysis of one-handed and two-handed tennis backhand strokes (M.A.) **361**

The code **340**

Cognitive processes in tennis players: test of three factors (Ph.D.) **469**

A comparative study of the effectiveness of four methods of teaching tennis (Ed.D.) **197**

A comparison of a computer method versus a traditional method of teaching beginning tennis (Ed.D.) **109**

A comparison of a self-directed learning approach to a traditional instructional approach in beginning tennis (D.A.) **229**

A comparison of an ideal tennis model and tennis performance (Ph.D.) **421**

A comparison of movement times between the open and the closed stance for the tennis forehand groundstroke (M.S.) **181**

Comparison of selected kinematic and kinetic parameters associated with the flat and slice serves of male intercollegiate tennis players (Ph.D.) **394**

A comparison of the effectiveness of two serving motions in tennis (M.A.) **147**

A comparison of the personality traits of participants and nonparticipants in high school interscholastic tennis programs for girls (Ed.D.) **280**

A comparison of the personality traits of tennis coaches (M.S.) **435**

A comparison of three different teaching aids on the improvement of the forehand and backhand strokes among intermediate tennis players (Ed.D.) **126**

Competitive tennis: a guide for parents and young players **25**

The complete beginner's guide to tennis   see: The complete guide to tennis (Lardner) **236**

Complete book of championship tennis drills **306**

Complete guide to tennis **77**

The complete guide to tennis (Lardner) **236**

The concise dictionary of tennis **170**

The construction of a test to measure perceptual ability in tennis for college women (M.S.) **176**

The construction of a volley test for aerial tennis (M.S.) **326**

The construction of forehand drive, backhand drive, and service tennis tests (Ed.D.) **98**

Contemporary tennis **332**

Count one! to top tennis technique **44**

Courtside companion: a tennis workbook for the serious player **501**

COURTSTAR program **445**

Covering the court **70**

Covert-overt service routines: the effect of a service routine training program on elite tennis players (Ed.D.) **302**

The dance of tennis **286**

Delayed augmented feedback: the usefulness as perceived by intercollegiate tennis athletes (Ed.D.) **472**

Dennis Ralston's tennis workbook **343**

Dennis Van der Meer's complete book of tennis **465**

Design B: how to play tennis in the zone **120**

Development and evaluation of a self-talk assessment instrument for tennis players (Ph.D.) **468**

The development of a test for assessing ability to serve in tennis (M.S.) **16**

The development of children's expertise in tennis: knowledge structure and sport performance (Ph.D.) **283**

Direct tennis **391**

Doctor tennis: a complete guide to conditioning and injury prevention for all ages **99**

A doctor's answer to tennis elbow: how to cure it, how to prevent it **185**

Title Index

The doctor's guide to better tennis and health **127**

Doubles strategy: a creative and psychological approach to tennis **107**

Drills for skills: a handbook for tennis players of all abilities **30**

Early environmental factors reported by amateur tennis players (Ph.D.) **132**

Ed Faulkner's tennis: how to play it, how to teach it **116**

The education of a tennis player **241**

The effect of a short-handed tennis racket on the acquisition of basic tennis skills (M.S.) **418**

Effect of ball velocity on spatial accuracy of the tennis volley (M.A.) **338**

The effect of continuous and interval step training on attitudes, cardiovascular fitness, and tennis skills of beginning tennis students (Ed.D.) **276**

The effect of music on the learning of tennis skills (Ph.D.) **490**

The effect of programmed instruction on selected tennis skills, knowledge and attitudes (Ph.D.) **129**

The effect of selected tennis racket and string variables on ball velocity and the force of ball-racket impact (P.E.D.) **239**

The effect of teaching aids on the performance of a selected tennis serve (P.E.D.) **175**

The effect of the graduated length method on tennis achievement of beginners (P.E.D.) **480**

The effect of two specific practice environments on the forehand and backhand ball placement ability of beginning tennis players (Ed.D.) **357**

The effect of utilizing shorty tennis rackets on beginning tennis achievement by college women (M.S.) **219**

The effect of videotape viewing training on learning tennis skills when utilizing videotape replay for feedback (Ed.D.) **171**

Effects of age and success on arousal levels of advanced female tennis competitors before and after tournament competition (M.Ed.) **162**

The effects of augmented visual cues on the performance of groundstroke consistency for beginning college-age tennis classes (M.S.)   **82**

The effects of forearm strength on laterial epicondylitis (M.A.)   **179**

Effects of velocity, surface, and angle of incidence on angle of rebound of tennis balls (Ph.D.)   **259**

The effects of videotape instant visual feedback on learning specific gross motor skills in tennis (Ed.D.)   **10**

An electromyographic study of ballistic movement in the tennis forehand drive (Ph.D.)   **5**

An electromyographic-cinematographic analysis of the tennis serve (Ed.D.)   **419**

Ellsworth Vines' quick way to better tennis: a practical book on tennis for men and women   **473**

The encyclopedia of tennis   **358**

The establishment of norms for two selected tennis skills tests at North Texas State University (M.S.)   **14**

The expert: an analysis of tournament play   **426**

Explanation paradigms: their application potential in the field of tennis instruction (Ph.D.)   **478**

Extraordinary tennis for the ordinary player   **345**

40 common errors in tennis and how to correct them   **384**

A factor analysis of selected tennis skill tests (Ed.D.)   **173**

The family tennis book   **313**

Fine points of tennis   **293**

Finding and exploiting your opponent's weaknesses   **237**

Fit for tennis   **356**

Focus on competition: a tennis manual   **388**

Forehanding and backhanding...if you're lucky   **324**

Friend at court   **339**

Fundamentals of tennis   **334**

Title Index

The game of doubles in tennis **412**
The game of singles in tennis **413**
Game, set, match...a beginning tennis guide **53**
Get fit for tennis **34**
Getting started in tennis (Ashe and Robinson) **12**
Getting started in tennis (Metzler) **294**
Ground strokes in match play: techniques, tempo, and winning tactics **19**
A guide to the literature of tennis **271**

A handbook for chairmen of junior tennis tournaments **446**
A handbook for junior tennis tournament players **447**
A handbook for planning and conducting tennis tournaments **27**
The handbook of tennis **101**
Harry Hopman's winning tennis strategy **183**
Hitting blind: the new visual approach to winning tennis **402**
Hitting hot: Ivan Lendl's 14-day tennis clinic **253**
How to beat better tennis players **118**
How to hire a tennis professional **438**
How to improve your tennis: style, strategy, and analysis **485**
How to increase your net value: a simplified guide to better tennis **389**
How to play better tennis **474**
How to play championship tennis **245**
How to play mixed doubles **216**
How to play power tennis with ease **190**
How to play tennis (Jones) **202**
How to play tennis (Sedgman) **378**
How to play tennis the professional way **436**
How to play winning doubles **266**

How to play winning tennis   **246**

How to play your best tennis all the time   **226**

How to succeed at tennis   **366**

How to succeed in tennis without really trying: the easy tennismanship way to do all the things no tennis pro can teach you   **289**

How to talk tennis   **369**

How to win at ladies' doubles   **69**

How to win at tennis   **225**

The ITCA guide to coaching winning tennis   **26**

I want to be a tennis player   **15**

If I'm the better player, why can't I win   **123**

Illustrated tennis dictionary for young people   **407**

Improve your tennis   **193**

Improving your tennis game   **148**

Improving your tennis: strokes and techniques   **203**

An individualized instructional approach to tennis   **392**

The influence of a modified racket on the learning of certain fundamental tennis skills by young children (Ed.D.)   **351**

The influence of programmed instruction on the achievement of specific skills in tennis (Ed.D.)   **2**

The influence of psychological stress and personality upon athletic performance of intercollegiate tennis players (M.S.)   **350**

The inner game of tennis   **130**

Inner tennis: playing the game   **131**

Inside tennis   **398**

Inside tennis for women   **189**

Inside tennis: techniques of winning   **252**

Instant tennis: a new approach based on the coordination, rhythm and timing of champions   **43**

Instant tennis lessons   **231**

Instructors: are they significant? (ERIC document) **135**

Instructor's manual, volume 2 **341**

An integrated skills reinforcement program for beginning tennis **402A**

Intelligent tennis: a sensible approach to playing your best tennis...consistently **390**

Intermediate tennis **137**

International symposium on the effective teaching of racquet sports. Proceedings, June 11-14, 1980 (ERIC document) **160**

An investigation of the interrelationships existing among psychological aggression, court aggression and skill in male and female intercollegiate tennis players (Ph.D.) **166**

Ivan Lendl's power tennis **374**

Jimmy Connors: how to play tougher tennis **79**

Junior tennis **251**

Ken Rosewall on tennis **359**

A kinematic analysis of the tennis one-handed and two-handed backhand drives of highly-skilled female competitors (Ph.D.) **156**

A kinematic comparison of selected measures between two different part methods and the full tennis serve motion (M.S.) **393**

The LTA guide to better tennis **9B**

LaCoste on tennis **228**

Lawn tennis as played by the champions **318**

Lawn tennis for club players **427**

Lawn tennis for young players **428**

Lawn tennis: how to become a champion **83**

Lawn tennis lessons for beginners   **319**
The lawn tennis library   see:
   Lawn tennis lessons for beginners   **319**
   Mechanics of the game of lawn tennis   **320**
   Methods and players of modern lawn tennis   **322**
   Psychology and advanced play of lawn tennis   **321**
Lawn tennis: the Australian way   **336**
Lawn tennis: the game of nations   **254**
Learn to play tennis at home   **483**
Learning tennis together   **108**
Learning to play better tennis   **247**
Let's play tennis (Davison-Lungley)   **91**
Let's play tennis (Stolle and Appel)   **403**
Levels of the game   **282**
Lifetime treasury of tested tennis tips: secrets of winning play   **310**
Load sharing in the forearm muscles prior to impact in tennis backhand strokes (Ph.D.)   **281**
Lobbing into the sun   see: Harry Hopman's winning tennis strategy   **183**
Love and hate on the tennis court: how hidden emotions affect your game   **67**

Mastering the art of winning tennis: the psychology behind successful strategy   **128**
Mastering your tennis strokes   **385**
Match play and the spin of the ball   **429**
Match point   **349**
Match-winning tennis: tactics, temperament and training   **204**
The mechanics of lawn tennis   **191**
Mechanics of tennis   **498**
Mechanics of the game of lawn tennis   **320**
The mental advantage: developing your psychological skills in tennis   **479**

Title Index

Mental toughness training for sports **261**

Methods and players of modern lawn tennis **322**

Mind, set, and match: using your head to play better tennis **57**

The "mini-match" as a measurement of the ability of beginning tennis players (P.E.D.) **163**

Mixed doubles tennis **150**

Modern tennis **194**

Modern tennis doubles **395**

More instant tennis lessons **232**

My guide to better tennis **36**

My life and game **37**

Muscle patterning in the overarm throw and tennis serve: an electromyographic and film study of skilled and less skilled performers (Ph.D.) **6**

Net results: the complete tennis handbook **96**

Net results: training the tennis parent for competition **262**

A new practical tennis book: strokes, strategy, and successful play **121**

Nick Bollettieri's junior tennis **32**

Nonverbal communication of winning and losing in tennis (Ph.D.) **481**

The on court book of tennis drills **90**

Operational procedures for implementing mastery learning in physical education (ERIC document) **172**

Optic yellow fever: treat tennis as a game and you'll get better **467**

Optimal tennis: the freeze-frame photographic approach to a better game **161**

Organization and conduct of tennis clinics and teacher training workshops **493**

Pancho Segura's championship strategy: how to play winning tennis **381**

The parent-player tennis training program **263**

Pattern play tennis **45**

Peaking through tennis: a mind/body guide to peak performances **58**

Peter Burwash's tennis for life **60**

A philosophical analysis of the relationship between the whole-man concept and tennis (Ed.D.) **140**

A photographic guide to tennis fundamentals **260**

Physical education: tennis, physical fitness, body-building (ERIC document) **471**

Play better tennis **304**

Play better tennis: 50 star tips **188A**

Play better tennis with Billie Jean King **212**

Play tennis with Rosewall **360**

The playboy book of tennis: how to play winning tennis **401**

Playing tennis **17**

Playing tennis when it hurts **61**

Power tennis **78**

Prelongitudinal screening of hypothesized developmental sequences for the tennis serve and the effect of sex, experience, and age on developmental level (Ed.D.) **291A**

Prime time tennis: tennis for players over 40 **382**

Principles of tennis: techniques, drills, and strategies **157**

Proceedings of a national symposium on the racquet sports: an exploration of research implications and teaching strategies, June 13-16, 1979 (ERIC document) **159**

Professional tennis drills **47**

Psych yourself to better tennis **273**

Psyching up for tennis **250**

Psychodynamic tennis: you, your opponent, and other obstacles to perfection **143**

Psychology and advanced play of lawn tennis **321**

Qualitative biomechanics and the tennis ground strokes (ERIC document) **113**

Quick tennis **177**

Quick tips from the CBS tennis spot **62**

Racket work: the key to tennis **20**

Racquet and paddle games, a guide to information sources **329**

Reactivity of efficacy evaluation and prediction on performance of women tennis players (Ph.D.) **114**

The relationship between the area of visual occlusion and groundstroke achievement of experienced tennis players (Ph.D.) **400**

The relationship of ball velocity and tennis playing ability of college men (P.E.D.) **375**

The relationship of mental image to skill performance in tennis (Ph.D.) **208**

Relationships between success in selected situations in tennis and the outcome of competition (M.A.) **64**

Relationships of forward hip rotation velocity, magnitude of forward hip rotation, and composite arm-shoulder strength to the flat tennis serve ball velocity (M.S.) **24**

Research and future directions for the study of motor skill acquisition and performance in aging populations (ERIC document) **362**

The resilient effects of three string tensions in seven different tennis rackets (M.S.) **297**

Returning the serve intelligently **265**

Rick Elstein's tennis kinetics with Martina Navratilova **111A**

Rod Laver's tennis digest (1973) **242**

Rod Laver's tennis digest (1975) **243**

The role of augmented knowledge of performance in the form of movement process correction in the acquisition of a motor skill (Ph.D.) **267**

Rules of tennis and cases and decisions **448**

The science of tennis **4**

Secrets of a winning serve and return **410**

A selected battery of tennis skill tests (Ph.D.) **387**

The serve and the overhead smash **370**

The serve: key to winning tennis **433**

Serving and returning service **94**

Simplification of TNT (Talent-N-Timing) test for college students (Ph.D.) **285**

Sinister tennis: how to play against and with left-handers **371**

The six insidious traps of college tennis and how to avoid them! **187**

Six weeks to a better level of tennis **344**

A skilled test and norms for the speed of the tennis serve (Ed.D.) **408**

Skills and tactics of tennis **305**

So you think you know tennis **86**

Solo tennis **494**

Special Olympics tennis sports skills guide **464**

Speed, strength and stamina: conditioning for tennis **167**

Sports Illustrated tennis (MacCurdy and Tully) see: Sports Illustrated tennis: strokes for success **279**

Sports Illustrated tennis (Talbert) **409**

Sports Illustrated tennis: strokes for success **279**

Stairsteps to successful tennis **470**

The Stan Garner tennis improvement method **133**

Stan Smith's guide to better tennis **396**

Stan Smith's six tennis basics **397**

Starter tennis **449**

Starting tennis **207**

The steady game **315**

Stroke production in the game of tennis **414**

A study of sex differences in locus of control, tennis expectancy for success, and tennis achievement (Ph.D.) **249**

Title Index

A study of sex role, sex differences, locus of control, and expectancy of success in tennis among college students (Ph.D.) **169**

Study of the cognitive plan in the acquisition of complex motor skill. Continuation of study I: good motor learners. Final report (ERIC document) **258**

A study to determine the relationship of selected physiological variables and playing ability of male collegiate tennis players (M.S.) **73**

Successful tennis: from beginner to expert in forty lessons **125**

Tackle lawn tennis this way **89**

Tackle tennis see: Play better tennis **304**

Tactics in women's singles, doubles, and mixed doubles **238**

Talent development: a study of the development of world class tennis players (Ph.D.) **299**

Teach yourself lawn tennis **84**

Teach yourself tennis **233**

The teachers' guide to urban tennis instruction. The New York City schoolyard tennis program. Pilot program, Spring 1984 (ERIC document) **420**

Teaching and coaching tennis **210**

Teaching children tennis the Vic Braden way **40**

The teaching of classical versus functional techniques in the acquisition of a tennis skill (Ed.D.) **155**

Teaching of tennis for school and recreational programs **196**

Teaching tennis **71**

The teaching tennis pro **248**

Teaching tennis with televised lessons: a comparative study of two teaching methods (Ed.D.) **65**

Teaching your child tennis **186**

Ten tests for better tennis **499**

Tennis (Barton and Grice) **22**

Tennis (Cutress) **88**

Tennis (Deflassieux) **95A**
Tennis (Douglass) **102**
Tennis (Gensemer) **138**
Tennis (Gonzales and Hawk) **145**
Tennis (Jacobs) **195**
Tennis (Johnson, Dewayne; Oliver, and Shields) **198**
Tennis (Johnson, Joan D. and Xanthas) **199**
Tennis (Johnson, M.L. and Hill) **200**
Tennis (Mabbitt) **275**
Tennis (McCormick) **277**
Tennis (Mason; Walts, and Mott) **287**
Tennis (Medlycott) **290**
Tennis (Pearce and Pearce) **327**
Tennis (Pelton) **330**
Tennis (Sebolt) **376**
Tennis (Seewagen) **380**
Tennis (Snyder) **399**
Tennis (Truman) **437**
Tennis (Wills) **484**
Tennis: a basic guide **354**
Tennis: a guide for the developing tennis player **54**
Tennis: a practical learning guide **75**
Tennis: a professional guide **439**
Tennis ability and its relationship to seven performance tasks (Ed.D.) **406**
Tennis and kids: the family connection **115**
Tennis and the mind **417**
Tennis and you **92**
Tennis, anyone? **149**
Tennis: back to the basics **500**
Tennis backhand strokes: a comparative study between the two-handed backhand stroke and the one-handed backhand stroke for beginning tennis players (M.S.) **288**
Tennis: basic techniques and tactics **95B**

Title Index

Tennis basics **230**

Tennis begins at 40: a guide for all players who don't have wrists of steel or a cannonball serve, don't always rush the net or have a devasting overhead but want to win **144**

Tennis: beyond the inner game **486**

The tennis book (Bartlett and Gillen) **21**

The tennis book (Cutler) see: Basic tennis illustrated **87**

Tennis by Machiavelli **346**

Tennis by simple exercises **255**

The tennis catalog **105**

Tennis charting: the graphic way **152**

Tennis clinic: play the TennisAmerica way **466**

Tennis: course proposal (ERIC document) **495**

The tennis doctor: everything you always wanted to know about tennis but didn't know whom to ask **264**

Tennis doubles: tactics and formations **295**

Tennis doubles: winning strategies for all levels **235**

The tennis drill book **331**

Tennis drills and skills illustrated **38**

Tennis drills for self-improvement **223**

Tennis drills: on-and-off-court drills and exercises for beginners, intermediate players, and teaching professionals **153**

Tennis: easy on - easy off **316**

Tennis everyone **301**

The tennis experience **373**

Tennis for advanced players and those who would like to be **158**

Tennis for anyone! **317**

Tennis for beginners (Duroska) **106**

Tennis for beginners (Murray) **311**

Tennis for beginning and intermediate players **325**

Tennis for everyone **368**

Tennis for everyone, with official USLTA rules **1**

Tennis for schools **363**

Tennis for teachers 103
Tennis for the bloody fun of it 244
Tennis for the coach, teacher, and player 119
Tennis for the mature adult 300
Tennis for the player, teacher and coach 309
Tennis for the university student from recreation to competition 489
Tennis for thinking players 308
Tennis for women 422
Tennis for women (Hovis) 184
Tennis for young champions 9
Tennis for your child 3
Tennis: game of motion 372
The tennis grand masters: how to play winning tennis in the prime of life 56
Tennis group instruction II 291
Tennis handbook 174
Tennis handbook and curriculum guide 234
Tennis: how to become a champion 205
Tennis: how to play, how to win 431
Tennis in a wheelchair 323
Tennis in pictures 314
Tennis: individualized instructional program 7
Tennis instruction for fun and competition 224
Tennis is an unnatural act 488
Tennis is for me 97
Tennis, keep it simple 218
The tennis league handbook 209
Tennis: learn to volley first 405
Tennis love: a parent's guide to the sport 214
Tennis made (somewhat) easier 337
Tennis Magazine see:
        Arthur Ashe's tennis clinic 11

Title Index

If I'm the better player, why can't I win **123**
Instant tennis lessons **231**
Jimmy Connors: how to play tougher tennis **79**
More instant tennis lessons **232**
Quick tips from the CBS tennis spot **62**
Teach yourself tennis **233**
Tennis and the mind **417**
The tennis grand masters: how to play winning tennis in the prime of life **56**
Tennis: how to play, how to win **431**
The tennis player's handbook **423**
Tennis strokes and strategies **424**

Tennis magic: playing with a full deck **352**

Tennis medic: conditioning, sports medicine and total fitness for every player **257**

Tennis my way **312**

Tennis: myth and method **476**

Tennis notes **477**

Tennis, play to win the Czech way **178**

The tennis player's diet: a guide to better nutrition on and off the court **168**

The tennis player's handbook **423**

Tennis: playing a winning game **335**

Tennis: playing, training, and winning **134**

Tennis programs for the disabled **450**

Tennis psychology **136**

Tennis return of serve study with visual analysis (M.A.) **342**

Tennis rules and techniques in pictures **52**

Tennis science for tennis players **48**

Tennis self-instructor **104**

Tennis simplified for everyone **475**

Tennis strokes and strategies **424**

Tennis: strokes, strategy, and programs **49**

Tennis tactics: match play strategies that get immediate winning results **154**

Tennis tactics: singles and doubles **415**

The tennis teacher's guide: group instruction and team coaching **222**

Tennis: teaching, coaching, and directing programs **50**

Tennis: the Bassett system **23**

Tennis: the decision making sport **39**

Tennis: the skills of the game **9A**

Tennis the Swedish way **404**

Tennis tips **240**

Tennis to win **213**

Tennis -- up to tournament standard **201**

Tennis USA Magazine see:
> Winning tennis: strokes and strategies of the world's top pros **139**

Tennis weaknesses and remedies **296**

Tennis without lessons **51**

Tennis without mistakes **110**

The tennis workbook - unit one: for beginners and advanced beginners **220**

The tennis workbook - unit two: for intermediate and advanced players **221**

Tennis your way **33**

Topspin to better tennis **63**

Total health tennis: a lifestyle approach **487**

Total tennis: the mind-body method **353**

Total tennis training **227**

Tournament tough: a guide to junior championship tennis **142**

Trabert on tennis: the view from center court **432**

Triples: a new tennis game **141**

Two-handed tennis: how to play a winner's game **278**

Title Index

USA tennis course **416**

The USPTA accounting, business and financial management handbook **444**

The USPTA complete guide to coaching **440**

The USPTA junior development manual **441**

The USPTA sport science and sports medicine guide **442**

The USPTA tennis professional's business manual **443**

USTA college tennis guide, 1988-89 **451**

The USTA guide to forming a community tennis association **452**

USTA guide to fund raising for community tennis associations **453**

USTA Instructional Series   see:

    Covering the court **70**

    Finding and exploiting your opponent's weaknesses **237**

    Returning the serve intelligently **265**

    The serve and the overhead smash **370**

    Sinister tennis: how to play against and with left-handers **371**

    Speed, strength and stamina: conditioning for tennis **167**

    Tactics in women's singles, doubles, and mixed doubles **238**

    Tennis drills for self-improvement **223**

    The tennis player's diet: a guide to better nutrition on and off the court **168**

    The volley and the half-volley: the attacking game **211**

USTA schools program tennis curriculum **454**

USTA score book for coaches **455**

USTA senior tennis directory **456**

USTA short tennis: leader's guide to short tennis intramurals **457**

USTA SPORTSTAR kit **458**

USTA tennis camp/clinic directory **459**

USTA tennis films **460**

USTA tennis in the parks curriculum **461**

USTA tennis publications **462**

Ultimate tennis: the pleasure game **377**

Unisex tennis **256**

United States Tennis Association official encyclopedia of tennis **383**

Use your head in doubles **164**

Use your head in tennis **165**

The utilization of mental practice in the learning of selected tennis skills (Ph.D.) **268**

Utilizing a 5 of 9 point tie-break as a determinator of playing ability for college male tennis players (P.E.D.) **367**

Vic Braden's quick fixes: expert cures for common tennis problems **41**

Vic Braden's tennis for the future **42**

The volley and the half-volley: the attacking game **211**

The volley method versus the ground strokes method of teaching beginning tennis (Ph.D.) **59**

Volleying and lobs **95**

Watch the ball, bend your knees, that'll be $20 please! **76**

Welcome volunteers **463**

What is tennis? **348**

What research tells the coach about tennis **151**

When do we get to play, coach? **124**

Why you lose at tennis **122**

A winning combination **8**

Winning tactics for weekend singles **146**

Winning tactics for weekend tennis **434**

Winning tennis **333**

Title Index

Winning tennis after forty **303**
Winning tennis doubles **100**
Winning tennis: strokes and strategies of the world's top pros **139**
Winning tennis: the Australian way to a better tennis game **379**
Winning tennis through mental toughness **274**
Winning weekend tennis **496**
Winning with percentage tennis: an expert's guide to smart court strategy **269**
Women's tennis: a historical documentary of the players and their game **272**
Women's winning doubles **28**
World Tennis magazine   see:
       The book of tennis: how to play the game **270**
       Rod Laver's tennis digest (1973) **242**
       Rod Laver's tennis digest (1975) **243**
       Tennis, keep it simple **218**

Yoga tennis: awareness through sports **68**
You can teach your child tennis: a 30 day guide to tennis readiness **217**
The young sportsman's guide to tennis   see: Beginners guide to winning tennis **192**
Your advantage: a textbook for students and teachers of tennis **491**
Your book of tennis **206**

SUBJECT INDEX

Many of the titles in this bibliography are basic instruction books. Such books contain fundamental information about the sport: proper grips, basic footwork, correct hitting techniques for groundstrokes, serves, volleys, lobs, and speciality shots. Therefore, elementary subject terms associated with teaching tennis fundamentals do not appear in the index. Readers looking for information on the basics of tennis are advised to browse through the bibliography and select titles appropriate for their particular needs.

The subject terms found in the index have been carefully selected to assist readers in identifying sources about specific or more advanced aspects of learning and playing the game.

The numbers following subject terms refer to entry numbers in the bibliography.

Academic skills, teaching of, **402A**

Adult players, **46, 144, 146, 224, 300, 336, 382**

Aerobics, applied to tennis, **137, 492**

Aggression (court), **166, 211, 237**

Anthropometry, of players, **81, 365**

Arm strength, **24, 179, 419**

Assignments (written), **7, 495**

Australian tennis, **336, 379**

Backboards, use of, **38, 270, 494**

Backswing, **23, 147, 190, 278, 404**
- loop, **42, 328**
- straight, **328**

Ball, flight of, **4, 334**
Ball, velocity of, **239, 259, 338, 375, 400, 497**
Ball machines, use of, **38, 124, 126, 400**
Ball persons, training of, **188**
Ballistics, applied to tennis, **5, 43, 155**
Bassett System, **23**
Bassin Anticipation Timer, **29**
Bausch and Lomb Vision Tester, **29**
Behavior modification, **274**
Bibliographies, **271, 329, 462**
Biomechanics, applied to tennis, **113, 158, 159, 328, 430, 441, 442, 465**
Black players, **12**
Bollettieri System, of instruction, **32**
Broer-Miller Drive Test, **351**
Broer-Miller Forehand-Backhand Drive Test, **59, 135**
Broer-Miller Tennis Achievement Test, **375, 400**
Broer-Miller Tennis Drive Skills Test, Shepard modification of, **357**
Broer-Miller Tennis Test, **10**
Business, aspects of tennis, **443, 444**

CBS Radio Network, **62**
Camps, **66, 401, 423, 459**
Careers, **66, 440, 485**
Cartoons, **36, 95B, 136, 389, 467**
Cattrell High School Personality Questionnaire, **280**
Cattrell Sixteen Personality Factor Questionnaire, **350**
Champion Board, use of, **126**
Charting, use of in matches, **152, 477**

Subject Index 169

Children, teaching of, 3, 40, 115, 186, 214, 217, 262, 263, 283, 351

Children's books, 9, 12, 15, 36, 80, 88, 89, 93, 94, 95, 95A, 97, 106, 182, 206, 230, 247, 251, 277, 294, 324, 333, 348, 349, 354, 359, 363, 380, 403, 404A, 407, 437, 475

Choking, 128, 142, 262, 353

Class organization, 71, 196, 222, 316, 420, 430

Coaches, characteristics of, 72, 435

Coaching, 20, 26, 50, 60, 71, 119, 124, 151, 210, 307, 309, 312, 330, 405, 430, 440, 455

College tennis, 25, 187, 451

Communication skills, 50, 216, 440, 481

Competition, 49, 134, 152, 159, 161, 162, 166, 282, 293, 299, 345, 347, 350, 386, 426, 468, 485
- children, 88, 97, 214, 349
- training for, 13, 25, 124, 142

Concentration, 4, 117, 131, 205, 274, 390

Conditioning, 99, 102, 167, 213, 257, 264, 287, 301, 312, 404, 424, 431, 500, 501

Confidence, 42, 57, 205, 274

Coordination, 43

Court
- design, 42, 80
- coverage, 70, 99, 195, 201, 360
- positioning, of players, 212, 304, 378
- surfaces, 46, 48, 87, 95B, 122, 146, 213, 266, 370

Crossword puzzles, 174, 392

Czech tennis, 178

Dance, applied to tennis, 286

Dekan Automatic Performance Analyzers, 181

Depth, perception of, 29

Diagrams (color), 90, 424

Dieting, 99, 167, 168, 432

Dictionaries, 170, 369, 407

Disabled players, programs for, **450, 464**

Dissertations (Doctoral)
- D.A., **229**
- Ed.D., **2, 10, 29, 65, 72, 98, 109, 126, 140, 155, 171, 173, 180, 197, 276, 280, 291A, 302, 347, 351, 357, 386, 402A, 406, 408, 419, 472, 497**
- P.E.D., **163, 175, 239, 367, 375, 480**
- Ph.D., **5, 6, 59, 81, 112, 114, 129, 132, 156, 166, 169, 208, 249, 259, 267, 268, 281, 283, 285, 299, 365, 387, 394, 400, 421, 468, 469, 478, 481, 490**

Doctors (sports), **34**

Doubles, **96, 100, 107, 235, 266, 295, 395, 412, 434**
- Australian formation, **121, 238**
- children's, **9**
- mixed, **87, 100, 118, 128, 150, 184, 215, 216, 238, 254**
- poaching, **118, 121, 409**
- with left-handers as partners, **100, 238, 246, 371**
- women's, **28, 69, 238**

Drawings (color), **11, 247, 396**

Drills, **18, 22, 30, 32, 38, 47, 53, 76, 90, 92, 108, 111A, 119, 124, 153, 157, 211, 223, 227, 235, 306, 331, 364, 500, 501**

Dyer Backboard Test, Hewitt Revision of, **351, 357**

Dyer Backboard Test (Revised), **59**

ERIC documents, **113, 135, 159, 160, 172, 258, 362, 420, 471, 495**

Electromyography, **5, 6, 419**

Emotions, control of, **67, 227, 417**

Encyclopedias, **74, 358, 383**

Environmental factors, **132, 299**

Equipment, **8, 49, 53, 138, 188A, 198, 236, 277, 301, 304, 423**

Errors, correction of, **41, 51, 65, 110, 174, 292, 319, 341, 384, 389, 396, 416**

Etiquette (court), **91, 251, 275, 287, 368, 383, 389, 447**

Exercises, **35, 61, 92, 111A, 131, 134, 167, 189, 255, 356**

Subject Index

Eye movement, **29, 402, 473**

Facilities, utilization of, **222, 420, 449, 454**
Feedback
 - computer, **109, 472**
 - visual, **10, 82, 171, 267**
Female players, **14, 29, 82, 114, 129, 147, 162, 163, 166, 176, 181, 208, 219, 280, 284, 285, 288, 291A, 299, 351, 355, 365, 408**
Films, used in teaching, **6, 112, 342, 355, 361, 460**
Fitness, **9A, 17, 34, 39, 142, 257, 276, 356, 430**
Footfaulting, **52**
Fundraising, **453**

Gamesmanship, **128, 274**
General Serve Problem Solving Model, **258**
Geometry, applied to tennis, **1, 121, 307**
Glossaries, **12, 22, 23, 51, 53, 54, 61, 66, 69, 71, 74, 75, 77, 80, 91, 92, 95B, 96, 97, 103, 104, 108, 111, 119, 125, 134, 136, 137, 138, 142, 153, 154, 157, 174, 182, 192, 194, 199, 221, 224, 225, 236, 248, 251, 260, 264, 270, 275, 289, 290, 305, 307, 309, 312, 314, 327, 330, 332, 368, 369, 381, 383, 389, 391, 392, 398, 399, 405, 409, 411, 420, 430, 434, 437, 439, 464, 470, 475, 476, 482, 489, 491, 495, 500, 501**
Goals, used in teaching, **57, 227, 263, 313, 332, 495**
Gottschaldt Embedded Figures Test, **112**
Graduated Length Method, of teaching, **199, 219, 287, 351, 418, 480**
Grand Masters, **56**
Grand Slam, **241, 245**

Handicapping, **31, 110, 313, 388**

Health programs, **99, 127**
Hewitt Comprehensive Tennis Knowledge Test, **229**
Hewitt Speed of Service Test, **147**
Hewitt Tennis Achievement Test, **197**
Hip rotation, **24, 497**
Hiring, of professionals, **423, 438**
History, of tennis, **9, 49, 74, 80, 198, 277, 348, 349, 358, 369, 383**
Hooks Tennis Examination, **197**
Howard-Dolman device, **29**

Ideal Tennis Model of Skill Elements, **421**
Images (mental), **208, 390**
Injuries, **264, 356, 423, 442**
- prevention of, **46, 61, 128, 227, 489**
- treatment of, **66, 127**

Instruction, methods of, **478**
- individualized, **7, 172, 392**
- lessons, **33, 44, 125, 186, 231, 232, 242, 243**
- programmed, **2, 129, 220, 221**
- self-paced, **104, 116, 174, 229, 233, 392**

Junior tennis, **142, 251, 262, 441, 442, 446, 447**

Kemp-Vincent Rally Test, **14, 367**
Kinetics, applied to tennis, **111A**

Ladders (tennis), **209, 388**
League play, **209, 388**
Lefthanded players, **244, 275, 336, 436**

Lefthanders, as opponents, **118, 296,** 371
Lesson plans, **7, 195, 222, 234,** 291
Lessons, value of, **57, 401, 423**

Male players, **14, 29, 73, 82,** 129, 166, **180,** 197, 285, 288, **291A,** 299, **351,** 362, 365, 367, 375, **394**
Margaria-Kalamen Power Test, **284**
Match preparation, **9B, 46, 188A, 202, 204, 274, 305, 366**
Medicine (sports), 159, 257, **441, 442**
Memorable matches, 21, **241, 245, 360**
Mental training, **35, 39, 57,** 115, **117, 131, 142,** 225, 226, 250, 261, **263,** 268, **279,** 308, **390, 417, 486, 487, 488**
Momentum, **227, 274**
Morphology, of players, **81**
Motor skills, **2, 10,** 159, 258, 267, **291A,** 362
Muscles, use of
  - backhand, 281
  - forehand, **5**
  - patterning, **6**
  - relaxation, 57
  - serve, **419**
Music, applied to tennis, **286, 490**

National Collegiate Athletic Association (NCAA), **25, 451**
Nutrition, **8, 32,** 168, 227, 257, **442**

Objectives, used in teaching, **7, 71, 172, 196, 198, 234, 392, 420, 495**
Officiating, **301, 339**

Padder tennis, **363**

Parents, as teachers, **217**
Parents, guidelines for, **3, 8, 25, 40, 49, 214, 262, 263**
Pattern tennis (style of play), **45, 371, 500**
Pearson Product-Moment Correlation Analysis, **29**
Percentage tennis, **20, 122, 213, 269, 314, 336**
Personality, of players, **280, 282, 350**
Peter Burwash International, **60**
Philosophy, applied to tennis, **140**
Photographs (color), **46, 79, 91, 101, 188A, 275, 290, 305, 324, 333, 366, 372, 378, 396, 397, 404, 437, 439**
Photographs (sequential), **9A, 106, 116, 139, 260, 304, 314, 318, 501**
Photography, used in teaching, **75, 161**
Physical education classes, teaching of, **82, 141, 149, 172, 174, 219, 229, 309, 325, 471**
Physics, applied to tennis, **4, 48**
Physiology, of players, **81, 127, 151, 159, 206, 284**
Playing, philosophy of, **37, 55, 140, 193**
Playing ability, prediction of, **73, 114, 163, 169, 173, 288, 326, 357, 367, 375, 406**
Playing ability, evaluation of, **75, 111, 158, 234, 343, 355, 387, 400, 454, 471**
Points, importance of, **64, 314, 389, 413**
Power, attainment of, **190, 304**
Practice, methods of, on-court, **8, 9A, 9B, 110, 145, 205, 207, 279, 287, 304, 390, 404, 424, 431, 501**
Practice, methods of, off-court, **35, 337, 483**
Pressure, handling of, **42, 122, 127, 203, 350, 442**
Programs, administration of, **49, 50, 151, 196, 209, 291, 445, 449, 452, 454, 456, 458, 461**
Promotional activities (team), **26**
Psychology, **4, 17, 49, 53, 117, 128, 130, 131, 136, 143, 228, 273, 321, 352**
  - coaching, **26, 50**
  - court, **55, 120, 346, 425**
  - competition, **46, 123, 274, 279**
  - training, **46, 479**

Racket
- design, **48, 239, 334**
- skills, **18, 20, 201, 344, 497**
- stringing, **48, 239, 297**

Reaction time, **48**

Rebound nets, use of, **38**

Recruiting, **26, 440**

Research, applied to tennis, **151, 159, 160**

Rewards, **18**

Round robin tournaments, **316, 367, 388, 455**

Rules, **1, 12, 52, 53, 74, 77, 138, 198, 220, 236, 251, 277, 325, 339, 340, 383, 399, 403, 447, 448**

Rhythm, **43, 235, 286**

Scoring, **138, 209, 251, 277, 301**
- Van Alen Simplified Scoring System (VASSS), **52, 77, 380, 398**

Senior players, **56, 118, 303, 362, 456**

Sex, differences in, applied to tennis, **159, 169, 249, 256, 291A, 442**

Short tennis, **137, 457**

Skills, acquisition of, **59, 135, 155, 171, 227, 234, 249, 258, 267, 268, 276, 298, 305, 418, 421, 478**

Skills, performance of, **208, 469**

Somatology, of players, **81, 365**

Special Olympics, **464**

Spin (ball), **9A, 9B, 70, 83, 102, 192, 195, 228, 296, 332, 429**

Sports College, (Leimen, Germany), **46**

Sportsmanship, **1, 8, 17, 26, 31, 440, 441**
- children, **97, 428**

Stationary Test, **357**

Strategy, **1, 9B, 49, 107, 121, 128, 139, 157, 164, 165, 183, 213, 215, 216, 227, 269, 287, 301, 325, 341, 381, 424, 431, 500**

Strength training, **101, 492**

Stroking
- analysis, **9A,** 19, 156, **188A,** 228, 240, 246, 281, 320, **328,** 376, 377, **498, 500**
- angles, **42, 48,** 70
- correction, 210, 292, 343, **416**
- diagnosis, **41,** 264, **416**
- preparation, **344, 414**
- techniques, 278, **294, 296, 301,** 310, 322, 341, 360, 372, **385, 414, 424, 427, 428,** 465, 473, **501**

Success, expectancy of, **169, 249**

Swedish tennis, **404**

Syllabi (course), **221**

Tactics, 18, **19,** 146, 154, 204, 207, 216, 226, 279, 305, 315, 366, **404, 415**

Talent-N-Timing (TNT) Test, **285**

Tanking, **262, 432**

Teacher training programs, 103, 149, 309, 439, 493

Teaching, methods of, 60, **103,** 109, 116, 126, 155, 159, 197, 291, **307, 309,** 466, 470, **491**
- forehand, 267
- groundstrokes, **59,** 135, **391**
- return of serve, **265,** 342, 410, **415**
- serve, 159, 175, 258, **291A,** 302, 355, 393, 394, 410, **415, 433**
- volley, **45, 59,** 135, 218, **338, 405**

Teaching, philosophy of, **9B, 20,** 103, 161, 234, 252, 256, 309, 311, 353, **425**

Team unity, **227**

Television, used in teaching, 65

Temperament, of players, **1,** 204, 225, 228, 262, 292, 293, **484**

Tempo (pace), **19,** 52, 142

Tennis elbow, **127, 185**

Tests, use of
- knowledge (written), 7, 18, 22, 86, 102, 104, 196, 229, 283, 307, 392, 399, **491, 495**

- skills, 18, 75, 176, 196, 198, 200, 220, 221, 283, 285, 449, 454
    - service, 14, 16, 98, 147, 180, 197, 387, 408
    - forehand, 98, 181, 197
    - backhand, 98, 197
    - volley, 326

Theses (Master's)
  - M.Ed., 162
  - M.S., 14, 16, 24, 73, 82, 176, 181, 219, 284, 288, 297, 298, 326, 328, 350, 355, 393, 418, 435
  - M.A., 64, 147, 179, 338, 342, 361

Throwing (overarm), 6

Timing, of strokes, 43, 44, 192, 337, 338

Topspin, 42, 63, 121, 294, 332

Toss (service), 394

Tournaments
  - conducting, 27
  - planning, 27, 446

Trainers (sports), 34

Training, methods of, 178, 204, 227, 264, 276, 305, 312, 366, 432, 441, 442

Triples, 141

Two-handed backhand, 46, 83, 133, 156, 278, 288, 332, 361, 397

Videotapes, used in teaching, 10, 171, 197

Vision (peripheral), 29

Visual acuity, 29

Visual phoria, 29

Volunteer workers, 49, 463

WCBS-AM (radio), 62

Weather conditions, 87, 95B, 213, 389

Wheelchair tennis, 323

Women's tennis, **87, 184, 189, 215, 238, 272, 312, 317, 386, 422, 482**
Workbooks, **220, 221, 343, 392, 501**

Yoga, applied to tennis, **68**